The Wisdom of the One Heart

WORDS OF LIGHT *and* INSPIRATION

PAM HAMPTON

li/e it
● PUBLISHING ●

First published in 2012 by:

Live It Publishing
27 Old Gloucester Road
London, United Kingdom.
WC1N 3AX
www.liveitpublishing.com

All enquiries should be addressed to Live It Publishing.

ISBN 978-1-906954-49-9 (pbk)

Let the light dance
through you
Let the love come
from you
to other people
and back
Let love hold you
in its hand
And in the silence
wait

CONTENTS

A Film of Love
Misunderstandings
Freedom and Closeness
Cats and Dogs
Lullaby
Love Flower
Tones
True Love
Young Love
Love's Beauty
Goodness
Fairy Tales
Dreams
All Ways
Moving On
The Boat
Change

Funny

Paradise

Wealth

Yours

Beloved

Peace

In Hiding

For You

Together

Why

Letting Go

Dancing

Self Knowledge

Love

May You

Rainbow

Radio Station

Come

Flowing

Everywhere

Peace and War

Crystal

Love All

Wings

Blessing

On the Fringe

Cuddles
Always
True Love
Love is Healthy
For Ever
Heart Shaped
Sleeping
Beauty
View from a Window
Just There
Light Rays
If
If Only
Vision
Stay
Be
Wow
Flowers
Big
The Look
Questions
Cleansing
Restoration
The Tree
Centred
Colours
Naming
Angel

Senses
Reality
The Light Within

One and All
Opening
Changing
Home Coming
Relatedness
Transmutation
Words of Love
All Knowing
Rest
Kindness
Fearless
The Return
There and Not There
Innocence and Maturity
The Gardener
Everywhere
Seeking
Love is All
Weep Not
Acceptance
You are Held

Faces
Whispering
Fear
Essence
Listen
A Depth
The Butterfly
Suns and Moons
The Diamond
Healing
Miracles
Sunny Day
Heaven and Hell
Opening to Love
Aliveness
Pure Love
It's Fine
Forever
For You
Enjoy
Boundaries
Irritation
Saints and Sinners
The Flame
Knowing
Melody
At One
Return to Love

Tomorrow
Whatever
Another, Yourself
Everything
No Separation
Time
A New Way
Be Who You Are
Healing the World
Come Back to Love
Sounds
Love is Love
Relax
The Key
Follow Love
Day to Day
All
Life's Way
Touching Love
Love is There
Appearances
All is Love
Sharing
Open and Closed
In Love
Oneness
Everlasting
The Light

Love Asks Nothing
Experiencing Love
Love's Power
You Are Never Alone
Born to Love
Love Cannot be Destroyed
Perhaps You Can Stay
Skipping into the Arms of Love
The Power of Love

FROM READERS OF
THE WISDOM OF THE ONE HEART

YVONNE Excellent. I want to read these to my yoga group.

AUDE It is very good. It brought up things I can reflect on. Certain ones touched me very deeply.

KAREN Utterly wonderful. I loved the simplicity, humanity and quirkiness, its variety and yet its constant message of love. I will be buying multiple copies, indeed in bulk!

JANE Beautiful, powerful words – a feeling of calm and being reassured –that I can accept all that I am – an inspiration to evolve into my true potential, both to be and spread love. At times I was reduced to tears but uplifted too. It's like a written Rescue Remedy.

GAY Beautiful – will have something to say to both those just starting on their journey and those who have travelled a long way. Some of it touched my heart very deeply, some made me smile. Your years of experience shine through.

SHEILA G. Lovely. Simple to read yet profound.

HELEN Profound writing – things I can relate to. I take it to bed with me to read and it comforts me.

JANICE It really moved me. What you call the One Heart, I call God.

JACKIE from a Women's centre, It's very healing.

SHEILA DYSON author of "*Everest, A Cockpit and Antartica, Three Dreams Fulfilled*" Messages from the angels. A beautiful, challenging, uplifting piece of writing. There are so many parts I have to sit and ponder over, but the writing has a profound quality to it.

ADRIAN G.R. SCOTT poet and author of "*The Call of the Unwritten*" "The Wisdom of the One Heart" is an extended poetic meditation on the bedrock of love. Pam names this the One Heart. She says, "The One Heart is forever: It is, always has been, always will be." For so many of us who suffer from the vicissitudes of our moods and the roller coaster that life can be, here we are offered the chance to plunge into the deeper mystery. Homespun wisdom flows out of the pages and each poem builds into a home for the broken and weary. If you are in need of love and how to open yourself to its ever present mystery this book is for you.

THANKS

Thanks, acknowledgements and everlasting love
go to
all the lovely people who gave helpful and incredible
feedback on the book
whose words reside in the book
and whose sentiments live in my heart

They are
Aude le Barazar, Gay Bejamin, Sheila Dyson, Sheila
Gilson, Jane Milward, Yvonne Newton, Helen
Osborne, Adrian Scott, Janice Speddings,
Karen Taylor and Jackie

Thanks to
Jane Milward for computer work and Lynn Cooper for
long term office support
and to my children Mark and Tina for being in my life
Huge thanks to
my husband Brian
my rock

for support on all levels, typing, computer work,
support with publishing, love and devotion
and for just being there
to Murielle for her amazing support and work with
publishing and all at Live It Publishing
who helped so wonderfully
to all who read this book
and all the fantastic authors
whose books fill the numerous book shelves
which line my walls

To all
the wonderful teachers, healers and therapists
who have helped me along the way
to guides, angels
and all "the gang" in other dimensions
without whom
I would not still be here and the book would not have
been born

And last, but not least
thanks
to the One Heart

FOREWORD

The words in this book, of the One Heart and love, came to me over a period of a few months. A good time was when my husband and myself spent two weeks in a cottage in Brittany. The words came, seemingly unbidden, when I was resting, working, eating, travelling and even woke me in my sleep. I wrote on whatever scraps of paper I had to hand because, unless captured immediately, the words were lost. At times I carried my notepad and pen wherever I went. I also remember asking my husband to bring me my notepad and pen when I was in the shower! And then suddenly, the words stopped. The work was done.

The book comes from the still small voice within, call it what you will. I feel I have tapped into the energy of unconditional love and what I call the One Heart, as well as my higher self, my own unconscious mind, the mass unconscious, my own stories and universal stories, knowings, happenings and wisdom. This has provided a diverse, yet synergistic view of body, mind and spirit and the state of human and womankind and love.

The stories are both my stories and those plucked from the ether. Apart from family members and friends, they do not knowingly relate specifically to anyone I know or have met. However some of the stories I wrote I felt that I did not personally know anyone with that particular situation. Then a few days later someone would appear who had a similar story to tell.

I feel I have also been lovingly guided by what I call "the gang", which includes the universal energy I call God, the angels and archangels, guides and teachers, and many other beings and helpers.

I am grateful for what I receive which is more than just words. It comprises feelings and knowings which are beyond words, but which seem to be conveyed to some extent within the words.

I watched the words as I wrote them, and after I had written them, I read them and also when I was feeling down. They had the effect of touching me deeply; uplifting me and sometimes making me smile. I hope they will do the same for you.

The words represent my particular philosophy and experience of love and the One Heart, in the moment they were written. There is always more to know.

You may or may not agree with them, but they provide points for you to ponder in developing or adjusting and/or accepting your own personal viewpoint, whichever is right for you.

INTRODUCTION

I feel there have been many times in my life when I have touched
the nature of universal, unconditional love and the oneness of all
in the One Heart.

Those which particularly stand out are my birth, a dream I had
when I was seven years old, a near death experience, a regression
into a past life as an Essene as well as my travels out into the
universe and meeting beings of light.

At the moment of my birth in India, my mum had been in labour
for four days and was completely out of it. She was not able to be
there for me and protect me. As a result, as I was born, I was aware
of and took in the whole of India. This ranged from the awe
inspiring, wonderful spirituality, wisdom and unconditional love
to the horrors and depravations of poverty, illness and violence
at a time of the uprisings preceding Independence and Partition
in India.

The rest of my life, for a long time, I veered between these seeming
opposites until gradually, and with effort and help, I found myself
at times in a place of wholeness which transcended all.

From the British Raj to a small mining village in England, from lavish attention and riches, to poverty, abuse and abandonment, from wanting to leave the planet to wanting to stay, I found that, for me, the key element was love, a love which finally pervaded everything.

I found that love in the most improbable ways.

From being very young I was subjected to some very nasty things, including what I called "the tortures", a result of prejudice and family patterns. When things got really bad I would go out of my body so it was as if it was not really happening to me, and play in green meadows with Jesus. Today this would be called disassociation. It was a means of survival. Now I have got in touch with, integrated and healed this part of me. However, the experience also put me in touch with that unconditional love again, which even today moves me to tears.

The next key element of my experience with true love was a dream I had when I was seven years old. I dreamed that I saw Christ on the cross. But I didn't just see him, I felt what he felt. This is difficult, if not impossible, to put into words, but there was an overriding sense of compassion and understanding, and so much more, alongside my own feelings of bewilderment, grief and fear and love. All was being held by love. At my young age I was overwhelmed and went downstairs to my parents. "It's only a dream", they said and gave me a drink and sent me back to bed. But I knew it wasn't just a dream and that I had been changed. It took me years to integrate the dream and understand it further.

Later, just into my thirties, after a bout of post natal depression, which was also an expression of unresolved trauma, I was sitting in the bath and my overriding feeling was, "I no longer want to be here." I left my body and travelled swiftly down a tunnel towards a brilliant white light which embodied unconditional love completely. The experience is in one of the poems. Yet again I had the experience of a love beyond measure; pure and totally without judgement or conditions, which overwhelmed me at first until I was able to make sense of it all. No one at that time talked about near death experiences. I had read nothing about it and didn't understand fully what had happened. I was afraid people would think I was mad.

By the way, as a child I was always ill and nearly died a few times. I don't remember any similar near death experiences, but I do know I was opened up further to non physical realms. These remained with me, though somewhat hidden and secret, alongside my normal life during my teens and early adult life, until later I got even further and deeper in touch with them again.

Eventually I spoke up about my experiences. I found people and teachers who understood. I learned how to leave my body at will and travel into other dimensions. First there was the so called astral plane, which we visit in our dreams and where we initially go after we leave the planet. It is the place of all our dreams and desires. It is what we expect it to be according to our faith, beliefs and so on. It is where we can meet our loved ones who have passed on and where we can meet our guides, visit halls of learning and realise so much more of what life is about.

Later, I went beyond, into different realms and universes and met with angels and masters, nature spirits and beings from other planets. I learned to understand the geometry of life and so much more. I touched many layers of love and understanding.

I read so many wonderful books which helped me ground and put things together that rooms became lined with bookcases.

I also enjoyed my day job as a science teacher until further ill health forced me to follow a different path and to learn more about myself.

At one time I studied with Vicky Wall, an amazing and awesome lady who created the wonderful Aura Soma colour oils. Whilst she was lecturing in the hall at White Lodge, I glimpsed yet again an image of being with Jesus and many other people, this time by the Sea of Galilee. I mentioned it to her and she told me I had been there. I must admit that I immediately dismissed what she had said as a bit far fetched, but I did wonder why she said it.

I also discovered that my personal aura colour was the rose pink/pink bottle which was called "love and light." On one occasion I looked at other people's colours and decided they were better than mine. I raised my hand and asked Vicky, "Are you sure I'm the rose pink/pink?" In front of hundreds of people she declared extremely firmly, "Yes you are, always have been and always will be." That was me told!

A few years later, I began on occasion to see inside people who were troubled and surrounded by darkness, a light which was so bright, that had I seen it for more than the fraction of a second I glimpsed it, I would have been blinded. I knew then, without a doubt, that the light of love is in everything and everyone no matter what are the external appearances.

Many years later, the presence of Vicky Wall nudged me to go and have a regression session, where I was shown a past life I had as an Essene. The Essenes were a group of people who helped prepare the coming of Christ. They supported him in many ways, both practical and in other ways, with his mission. At the crucifixion many gave support by meditating in caves nearby, in other ways and some near the cross too. Within the community, I was called the One Heart. As a very young woman, I witnessed the crucifixion, as Vicky had previously told me. I felt the fear and danger all around me and also grief for what was happening to him, along with the incredible love he always gave, just like I had in my seven year old dream in this life.

Don't get me wrong, I don't think in any way whatsoever that I'm the only person in touch with the One Heart and unconditional love, if I'm even that at all. However I can connect with it in certain ways so far, which I want to share and share my own particular journey of how I got there. But of course everyone, and I mean everyone, ultimately has their own path, their own realisation of and their own connection to unconditional love and the One Heart. They just have to know it. In The One Heart we're all the same, and different too. I'll meet you there!

A long time ago, when I was first unfolding, I started teaching groups about what I called "self nurturing" and I learned as I went along. I began to read countless, wonderful books. I developed and healed myself, boy was I initially in a bad state, and then helped others to do the same for themselves. I remembered all the experiences and beings I had been in touch with as a child and it all opened up for me so much more. I studied with gifted teachers and trained in various therapies.

And so, in time, I found myself writing about the One Heart. The words came to and through me very quickly, and I watched as I wrote. I then checked them out to make sure they made sense and had come from the right place, of light and love.

The words and the feelings that came with them have given me great help, support and joy at times when I was sorting through and feeling the most difficult of situations, as well as ordinary times and happy times.

I share these words with you, with love and from the One Heart.

THE ONE HEART

What exactly The One Heart is cannot be fully explained in words, any more than a definition of God or love or nature can truly define the full experience of these things.

However, the One Heart is an understanding that we are all one, that the God like energy of unconditional love beyond what we as yet can fully comprehend; the Spirit within, is in everything and everyone. As such, although we would certainly never condone the negative actions of some members, there is at the same time unconditional love for all, in the same way that a parent may discipline a naughty child but also utterly and completely love that child.

The words in this book, if read and listened to from the heart, evoke healings and experiences of The One Heart.

REFLECTIONS ON LOVE
AND ON RELATIONSHIPS

*Poetic reflections on love, some of the
situations we face in our relationships
and some funny quirky reflections on
love and what we call love*

A Film of Love

Coming soon
To a cinema near you
The One Heart
Let go of your fears
Your prejudices and judgements
Your ignorance and pride
As you watch
Spellbound
And be transported
To a totally new
Dimension

ॐ ॐ ॐ

Misunderstandings

I love you I said
I like you a lot is what you heard
I want to be with you always said I
You'll be with me until you move on you heard
I said *I'll do the dishes*
You heard *I'll feed the fishes*
May I sit here said I
I'm sitting here is what you heard

I'd like us to have babies I said
I don't want any babies you heard
I looked into your eyes
and silently said *I love you*
You returned my gaze
and felt that I loved you

Freedom and closeness

The child held the cat
And the cat jumped out of her arms
Love is freedom said the cat
The child held the dog
And the dog wriggled in her arms
and licked her nose
Love is closeness said the dog
The man held the woman
Are you a cat or a dog
he asked

Cats and Dogs

Sometimes a cat and a dog
usually sworn enemies
Get together and form a bond of love and affection
Which is so good to see
and reminds us
That maybe it is possible that we too
can get together
with our sworn enemies
And form a bond
of love and affection

Lullaby

I sing you a lullaby
A lullaby of love
As you close your eyes gently
And drift into slumber deep
May the oceans of love carry you
To where the blue sky
Shines on you in rapture
And the white birds fly
Enclosed in your cloak

Of soft pearly down
Feet clothed in suede sandals
Jewelled bracelets on your arms
Your hair flowing loose
In tendrils fine and fair
As your dreams take you swiftly
To the island of love
And there you are greeted by the sunshine
king and queen
Who with open arms great you
And a huge cup of tea
And you sail down the river
Serenaded by love's young dream
Who sings to you softly
A lullaby of love

Love Flower

The little flower
lifted her face to the sun
No words passed between them
But she knew
she was loved

Tones

He spoke words of love
in a harsh voice
and she recoiled
He spoke harsh words
in a gentle way
and she was comforted

True Love

I mean to give you love
And harsh words come
out of my mouth
I mean to comfort you
But the pain beneath my words
betrays us both
I mean to show you
how much I love you
But my fear holds me back
I mean to hold you in my arms
But my doubts
keep my arms by my side
Only when I can go beyond

my anger, pain, fear and doubt
Can I really love you

Young Love

He yodelled
I love you
And the mountains
reflected back
All the eager yearning
in his heart
For Love

Love's Beauty

Let me speak to you
Of oranges and figs
And dancing lively jigs
Of happiness unbounded
Caring, sharing, laughing

singing
Of music quite celestial
Playing and sunbathing
Long leafy walks
And sun drenched beaches
Roses, violets and buttercups
Perfumed balmy evenings
Babies sweetly gurgling
Harvest time
Celebrations
Sumptuous food
Of friendship and family
Beauty and serenity
Peaceful calm and sleepiness
Wonderful togetherness
Bright colours shining
Joy of life and sailing
Drifting clouds
And dazzling whiteness
Angel's wings and bouncing
All these lovely things and more
We give to ourselves
When we love
Ourselves

Goodness

When things get too much
Go out to play
and bathe yourself
in the wisdom of children
As you soak in the bath
with your smelly things
Or walk through the woods,
or on the beach
with your hoop la
Sing tra la la
The world is good
And so am I

Fairy Tales

Beauty and the beast
The beast transformed by a kiss
into a prince
A fitting match
for the beautiful princess
A wonderful analogy
of love

Have you kissed the beast in you
today
Or have you screamingly kicked it
abandoned it
put it out of your heart
refused to understand it
and its beauty within
Why not blow it a kiss
right now
And while you are about it
How about kissing Snow White awake

Dreams

In the soft lullaby of dreams
a candle burns
a light exquisitely perfumed
And a bird's feather
flutters softly
to the green, green grass
And the red and yellow flowers
fold their petals
to the pink glow of the sky
As the humming insects settle

and soft furry animals
burrow deep
into their burrows
And the leaves gently rustle
in the darkening sky
Of rest, repose
and slumber
As hearts open
into dreams of love

ॐ ॐ ॐ

All Ways

The top and bottom of it
And the inside out
The warp and weft of it
And the round about
The up and down of it
And the side to side
The in and out of it
And the upside down
The near and far of it
And the far and wide
The round and round of it
And the way, way out

Every bit of it
The whole darn shout
Is love

Moving On

I forgive you, he said
Thank you, she replied
I accept what happened
That's nice
I understand why you did it
I appreciate that
Lets move on, together
They did

The Boat

Sailing on a sea of love
The water calm and peaceful
Sailing on an ocean of love

The water's pretty choppy
Sailing on the oceans of love
Riding the stormy waves
Sailing on the tide of love
In and out, out and in
Sailing into the harbour safe of love
Home again

Change

No, I shouted
I will not stand this any more
Change or leave
Things changed
And love walked in

A FEW SHORT LINES

A few short lines on love. You may wish to use these first thing in the morning to set the tone for the day, or at any time randomly pick one which is right for you at that moment

Funny

Isn't it funny
How laughing opens the heart
And crying sometimes does that too

Paradise

When everyone has known
What it is
to be in The One Heart
There will be
Paradise on Earth

Wealth

The One Heart is not poor
Or hazy and lazy
It is rich in the abundance
Of love

Yours

You ask *what is the One Heart*
The One Heart is yours

Beloved

Beloved, I say unto you
Thou art love
in the making

Peace

Peace, peace, peace, peace
Love, love, love
You

In Hiding

Search for me high and low
Look for me in the most unlikely places
And when you have found me
Tell everyone you know
Love can be found in the most unexpected places

For You

If you recognise yourself
in these pages
I had no one in mind when I wrote
Shout Hooray
Jump up and down
And give yourself
a pat on the back
For love

Together

See the light and love you are
Be the light and love you are
And acknowledge it in each other

Why

Why is love so often abused
Why are we so afraid of who we are
Why do we wall off, push away
the essence of love
Why do we find love so painful
at times
Why do we ask so many whys

Letting Go

Put your head upon my shoulder
Let me take away your pain
Let go and let love
Let go and let love
Let go and let love

Dancing

As love dances with you
Through the daffodils
Stand on tippy toes and reach for the stars

Self Knowledge

She looked into the eyes of love
And she saw herself there
But she did not recognise herself
For a long, long time

Love

Let love, love
And love love
Lovingly
Loving lovingly
And love lovers
All love
Love all

LOVE

May You

May your hopes for
love be rewarded
May your dreams for love be realised
May your passion for love be experienced
May your desire for love be manifest
May your love for love be
In the One Heart

Rainbow

She found the golden pot
At the foot of the rainbow
Opened it
And love came out

Radio Station

Quieten your mind
And listen
Really listen
And you will hear love
Keep your radio
Always attuned
to the station
of love

Come

Love is always there for you
Whenever you ask
Be peaceful in your heart, mind and soul
Come to me
The One Heart

Flowing

Sometimes the words flow on and on forever
Saying the same thing, but differently
Saying different things, the same
That is how it is
So that you will know
You will know
Love

Everywhere

On a beach
of pure white sand
Palm trees and blue lagoons
Love is
In the deep, dark dungeons
In a prison cell
Love is
Love is everywhere – just look for it
And you will find it

Peace and War

A heart divided
Is a heart at war with itself
In the one heart
There is peace

Crystal

The pink
of the crystal
of the crystal, the crystal, the crystal
Of love,
of love, of love, of love
Its being is powerful
beyond measure, measure, measure
The love
of God, of God, of God

Love All

The orphaned child
The starving beggar
Have need of our love
Can we love them all, each one
Yes, if we hand it over to love
The love in our hearts
The one true love

Wings

Fly
With the wings of a butterfly
The wings of a bird
And the wings of an angel
Into the transformation
The freedom and the glory
Of the One Heart

Blessing

Oft times
That which is not love in you
Comes to the surface
To be healed and/or released
This is not always easy
Bless it
With love

ॐ ॐ ॐ

On the Fringe

Sometimes when we connect
with the One Heart
We go out on a limb
We go where few have gone before
We go where we have never gone before
Others may react
Think we're strange
We don't fit in with what they know
Well, that's OK

Cuddles

Cuddle up
Let love enfold you
Feel its warmth against your skin
Know its comfortable presence
And rest a while

❦ ❦ ❦

Always

May I be so bold
As to tell you
You are always, always loved
Always, always in my heart
The One Heart

❦ ❦ ❦

True Love

A huge well of love
A heart of love
Which desired nothing
Except to be itself
To be what it truly was
Pure love
A One Heart
Of nothing but love

Love is Healthy

A baby that is loved
Is a baby that is beautiful
healthy and fit
A mind that is loved
Is a mind that is beautiful
healthy and fit

For Ever

The learning and growing never stops
Evolution continues
Even when you have reached
and are in the One Heart
There are even finer levels
of love
To experience and know

Heart Shaped

The heart shape is universal
Recognised everywhere
Beyond boundaries
of race, creed and politics
Beyond language
and separation of any kind
In all walks of life
And so is love

Sleeping

In the night time before you sleep
You might ask to be in the One Heart
And in the morning
when you awake
You may remember
being in the One Heart
and give thanks

Beauty

Beauty is akin to love
When we know our own beauty
No matter what we think we and our lives
look like
Then we will share in that beauty
And also share that beauty with everyone
What a beautiful world!

View from a Window

I sit at my window
and what do I see
I see the world
looking back at me

❦ ❦ ❦

Just there

Do not grieve dear one
Do not despair
Love is always
and ever there

❦ ❦ ❦

Light Rays

When your heart is heavy
Light rays of love will lighten it
Again and again and again

If

Sometimes she dreamed
of a prince
who would change her life
completely
with a kiss
Then she stopped dreaming
and changed her life
herself
And along came a prince
She had choices...

❦ ❦ ❦

If Only

He could not love her more
As she walked out the door
If only he'd told her before

❦ ❦ ❦

Vision

If we could see love
What would it look like

Stay

The One Heart
IS JUST BEAUTIFUL
I will be in it today

Be

Be at peace
Be free
Be lovely
In your heart
Now and always

Wow

Love has many forms
And yet, in itself
It is formless

Flowers

A rose is love
so is a dandelion

Big

When you think of the One Heart
Think Big

The Look

Dear Lord
When you look into my eyes
My heart is awakened

♥ ♥ ♥

Questions

What ever the question
The answer is love

♥ ♥ ♥

Cleansing

The gentle rain
Washes away pain
Bringing laughter
And sun ever after

Restoration

What ever scars
you have acquired
accumulated
and stored
in body, mind and spirit
It is through forgiveness
you will be healed
and restored to love again

The Tree

A tree spoke to me
Let me heal you with my love
So that you may find rest
A tree spoke
Thank you

Love is just a tear away

Centred

Beyond the anger and tears
Beyond forgiveness
There is nothing to forgive my dear
For all is happening as it should
As you balance your energies
And centre into love

Colours

Black and white, shades of grey
Duality
Golden white, like shining sun
The One Heart

Naming

I call you by name
And your name is love
I am love
calling love

Angel

Let the angel of love
enfold you in her wings
of soft downy feathers

Senses

I flew into the arms of love
and rested there for a while
I looked into the eyes of love
and saw myself reflected there
I felt my way into the heart of love

and no longer felt separation
I walked with the feet of love
into a new world

ॐ ॐ ॐ

Reality

Sometimes you think
you are afraid of love
It is not love you fear
but what you think
are its consequences
In reality
The consequence of love
Is Love

ॐ ॐ ॐ

The Light Within

You ask me for beauty and love
For words in clichés
which make sense
which are comfortable
Can you not see the beauty and love
behind the uncomfortable words
of chaos and ugliness and hate

MESSAGES OF LOVE

A selection of short messages to bring you comfort, inspiration, peace, joy and sometimes challenges to reflect on and develop your own understandings of what is love and what is not love

One and All

In the One Heart
There is no you and me
No friend and foe
No victim and aggressor
No black and white
There are none of these
And yet they are all there
In The One Heart

ॐ ॐ ॐ

Opening

The One Heart
is beyond me right now
It beckons my own war torn
one dimensional heart
to open to being encompassed
by it's eternal love
To heal, to love again
To be strong

Changing

I walked down to the river
and sat there for a while
A long while
And then I walked back
to where I was before
I walked to the river
Except
it was not the same place
as it was before
It had changed
For so had I

ॐ ॐ ॐ

Home Coming

The One Heart
Where is it
It is everywhere and nowhere
Do not go out hunting
Stay at home
For home is where the heart is
And The One Heart is
Home

Relatedness

The physical heart is made of
auricles and ventricles
muscle of a particular kind
molecules and atomic particles
The One Heart is made of
energy of a particular kind
Are they related
Yes
The One Heart is related to everything
The world
The universe
Man and womankind
God, the Universe, one's Higher Self
It is relationship
In action
To the ultimate

Transmutation

May all that you fear
be transmuted into love
May all that you hate and loath

be transmuted into love
May all that you despise and judge
be transmuted into love
May all that you think, feel and know
be transmuted
For evermore
Into love

Ascend to The One Heart
On wings of gold and white

ॐ ॐ ॐ

Words of Love

Sweetheart, love heart, warm heart
Strong heart, lion heart, heartened
Heart beat, heart transplant, heart muscle
Giving heart, compassionate heart, heartfelt
Golden heart, white heart
Open heart, full heart, light heart
Healing heart, heart centred, heartsease
Heartbroken, heartless, cold heart
Black heart, hard hearted
Closed heart, no heart, leaden heart
Disheartened, bleeding heart, heart of stone

Many hearts
One Heart

All Knowing

The One Heart
is love
Pure love
Say the words
Over and over
to yourself
Love, love, love, love, love
And you will know
The One Heart

Rest

Rest in the peace
of the One Heart
Now and always

Forever
I will always be with you
Always
Even unto the end
of the world

Kindness

Benign
Is a word to describe
someone
who does no harm
Do no harm
and come to me
Let me enfold you
in love
A heart which is benign
Now and always
Amen

Fearless

Be not afraid
Love cancels out all fear
How is this
Because in the heart
Where there is room only for love
Fear exits

The Return

When you come into yourself
and own yourself
You start dancing and singing
and I am well pleased
and happy
that you are happy and well
When you deny yourself
and do not love yourself
nor dance and sing
But lie down
unwell
unhappy
I am with you

Until you return to yourself
and happiness once more
and together we can sing
and dance

ॐ ॐ ॐ

There and not There

I am there in your laughter
Like the tinkling water of a mountain
stream
as it flows over the
rocks
Or a great sonorous boom
a rumbling in the belly
and a falling over with mirth
A short sharp snort
or a giggle behind a hand
An open bellow of delight
A joyous melody
resonating through your body
and the air
A harmony of laughing notes
But when you snigger and smirk
at someone else's expense

or your own
When the cynical, cackling
witch's heart
escapes your lips
Or the barely hidden sneering
snort behind the hand
is there
Then I am not there

ॐ ॐ ॐ

Innocence and Maturity

Babies know me
baby humans
baby tigers
baby fleas
baby every things
They express me, my love
just by their being
And all respond
But when the world gets its sticky fingers on them
And things happen
I am lost
to the children
and those around them

However when innocence and love
is eventually regained
Through willingness and effort
It is so much more
mature
wise
fulfilling
Well worth working and
waiting for
It is not this way
just to be difficult
It is so love will grow

The Gardener

Maybe I will come to you tonight
Maybe I will come to you as you lie dreaming
And in your dreaming, plant a seed of hope
That will incubate for a while
And then spring into your consciousness
Seemingly unasked for
But there nevertheless
What will you do with it
Destroy it

banish it as an unwanted thought
Or tend to it
water it
nurture it carefully
and with love
The choice is yours dear one
We watch and wait
with infinite patience
Until you are ready
To be the gardener
and the harvester
of your soul

Everywhere

Imprinted in these words
are the seeds of love
Imprinted in these words
is the beingness of love
Love will touch you
You will be touched by love
And then anything can happen
my dear
But whatever happens

Know that it is love
And you have nothing to fear
Letting go of fear
is letting in love
You are love
You are love
Love is near
Behind you
In front
Above
And below
All around
All within
Love
Love
Love

seeking

Let us be very clear about love
Love is not all mushy or romantic
or blind
or obsessive
or kind

or sexy
or straight
or whatever
all these of course are aspects
or expressions of love
in some way
And there are many more
The reality of love
Cannot as yet be fully comprehended
But you are on your way
on your way
Seek and you will find is a truism here
But when you do find
You cannot give it to some one else
Only be with them
in their seeking
And when two or more begin to find
the reality of love
And join together in a relationship or a group
Then something wonderful happens
Seek and you will find
what it is

Love is All

What is considered to be law in one country
Is not the law in another country
What is considered to be religious by one
Is not the religion for another
Beyond these disparities
The glue that holds them together
is love
But it is not quite as simple as that
To unite with your fellow woman and man
You must let go of fixed ideals
which are set in stone
Which support and comfort you
because you have known them as a child
or been converted
See the light which shines
in all laws and religions
Go for that
And let all else
fall by the wayside
And only pick it up again
if it helps you
and those around you
Beloved
Be love
Which is beyond race
creed

denomination
woman and man made laws
Which is a part of everything
Be in the One Heart which encompasses all laws
religions
races and creeds
And yet is not any of them
Love stands alone and
Love is all

Weep Not

Weep not for me
For I am love
I weep for thee
Fear not for me
For I am love
I fear for thee
Love me
As I love you
And in the end
You will know
There is no separation
No gulf that divides us
We are one

Acceptance

I asked a group of people
Who in your life, is it most difficult to forgive
For each and everyone
The answer was
Myself
Why are we so hard on ourselves
Why do we judge ourselves the most harshly
Why do we expect ourselves to be perfect
Can we turn this around
Right now
Choose to let go of all our misdemeanours
Both large and small
Banish guilt and shame
And if we can't do it ourselves
Can we at least say
I am willing
And let love do the rest
So that we can be at peace
with ourselves
And rest
at ease
in the One Heart
Once and for all

You are Held

I tuck you up in bed at night
I kiss you when you wake
I hold your hand through the ups and downs
Of each and every day
And when at last you see me
And speak my name
That is when I enfold you
In wings of perfect love

Faces

As you face the trials and tribulations
of your life
Lift your face
to face the light and love
which is pouring forth now
onto the face of the earth
and the faces of all those
who dwell on her
Let your light shine
as you face each other
Radiant with love
For ever

Whispering

Some of you are involved with
what is called horse whispering
We would like
all of you
And others too
Now, to whisper to yourselves
Words of love, of wholeness
of encouragement
Just as we whisper them to you
all of the time
So that you may grow in love
Demonstrate love in the world
Heal yourselves and others
from all that is not love
And be for ever blessed
in the One Heart
of love

Fear

Be not afraid when darkness is near
Be not afraid of who and what you fear

But if you are afraid
Then let love be near
Affirm it until you feel it
Let love transmute fear
Let love be the key
To letting go of fear
Let Love be your sword and shield
As you face fear
And become more and more
Wholly Love

Essence

The essence of love is clear
it has a purity
The essence of love
holds everything and everyone
The essence of love is a spark
of Divinity
Love in its essence is a
creative force
The One Heart holds the
essence of love
From the beginning of time

until eternity
The essence of love
is in you
You are the essence of love
in reality

Listen

If you stop and listen
really listen
And wait patiently
for a long or short time
If you trust and believe
yourself and what you hear
If you sift out the truth from the untruth
In the silence
Love will answer
And you will know love

A Depth

His eyes were deep pools
Into which you could dive

But as you dove deeper
You found yourself spinning
Round and round
Out of control
Deeper and deeper
A flash of light
And then
Peace, perfect peace
Inestimable love

ॐ ॐ ॐ

The Butterfly

There is a transcendence going on
A transmutation of energies
into a new dimension
Love in a new dimension
is nothing like
the love you know now
It can not be described easily
in words
But if you continue
with your metamorphosis
Do the work
Let go of what you need to let go

Heal and transmute all that needs
to be healed and transmuted
Continue with your evolution
And dedicate yourself to
your mission
your work with and within the light
Then there is no doubt
that the caterpillar will turn into
the butterfly
And know love

Suns and Moons

Many moons
and many suns
will pass
Before you know yourself
completely
as love
Let each moon
and each sun
Escort you and
light your way
So that the way

also
Is filled with
Love

கு கு கு

The Diamond

Put love on the edge
the periphery of all that you do
and are
And you become a Jack of all trades
a dabbler in a fragmented love
Put love at the centre
and you become at once
a multi-faceted diamond
Steadfast
and loyal
Strong and
centred
Bright and shining
Powerful
in your love

Healing

If it has always been your way
to be critical and judgmental
of yourself and others
It will take time for you to adjust
to a new way of being
Your old habits and thoughts
will be threatened
with the thought of extinction
With losing face by being thought wrong
With insecurity, confusion and fear
of the new, seeming opposition
Be patient and kind to yourself
and your thoughts and fears
Allow the new
the unconditional love
to hold all the fear and doubt
Until it is ready to be loved
Stay steady and centred
and firm in your resolve
To heal all that is not love
With love

Miracles

When the one heart embraces you
Allow it
Soften tired, pain filled muscles
Will them to open to
the healing power
of love
Then you will know
what it is
To know that miracles
can happen
Even if the miracle is just that you live with love
In your body and mind
And that can lead to anything and everything

Sunny Day

Everything is wonderful
On a fine summers' day
And love fills all the spaces
where we hope and pray
It really isn't much to ask
To want to be happy

and joyful and free
So lift your face to the sun
And allow it to be
Smiling and dancing
And other ways of fun
Laughing and joking
The journey has just begun
And serenity smiles
her love all around
So witness together
A love most profound

Heaven and Hell

Hell is empty of love
Heaven is full of love
Hell is where there is no love
In heaven love is everywhere
Hell is all that is not love
Heaven is all that is love
Heaven, Hell
You choose
Choose lovingly and you have heaven
Choose without love and there is hell

But if you choose the latter
Even the smallest thought of love
Will be a stepping stone out of hell
And towards heaven

Opening to Love

The One Heart is wise
It carries a wisdom all of its own
When we open our hearts
We begin to act, feel, think more wisely
We set aside petty gains, conflicts, despair, fear
And thousands of impediments which block our way
to the free flow of love
Love without question
Love without condition
Love that expresses itself in ways
that support, help and enlighten
All

Aliveness

The One Heart is
Alive
It runs through the forests
of the mind
of all man and woman kind
It kindles the desire
to be at one
with all that is
It lights up the skies
of your very being
It is at home with the energy of
Love
It flows through the rivers of
your heart
It is alive with
your beingness
the God within
Live it, love it
Be Alive

Pure Love

All we ask
dear one
Is that you
let go
and
relax
into love
Pure love
without conditions
Always
Even when
there is the presence
of not love
also in your heart
Let the one
hold the other
until there is
harmony and peace
The bringing together
of polarities as one
The One Heart

It's Fine

And no more songs
And no more dances
In the world of hate and repression
Which is in your very cells
And comes to your awareness
at times
What do you do
Do you hold on to it
or let it go
Do you love it or hate it
Do you give it space
or suppress it
Do you defend yourself
against it
Or do you do all of these things
This is fine
Whatever you do is fine
And when you understand that
You will be at one with yourself
And know yourself as
The One Heart

Forever

The One Heart is forever
Do you know what that means
Forever
Forever is for always
No never
No polarity
Just circular
On and on
Forever and ever
That is how real love is
Do not be afraid of it
Or think that when you slip back
Into duality
And polarity
That it is gone
Because it can never do that
It is forever

For You

Some of my words
The words of the One Heart

May not make sense to you
You may try to order them
in your mind
Relate them to what you know
and how you know
Put them into your frame of reference
This may work
or may lead to frustration
a throwing down and condemnation of the words
If instead
you allow them
to speak to your soul
Listen
without judgement
or even needing to know
Allow them to caress you
Wash over you in waves
Let them be
in the silence of your knowing
Then little by little
or all at once
The loving
will come
to you

Enjoy

See with loving eyes
Love what you see
Both good and bad
Hear with loving ears
Relax into the beautiful and the harsh
Taste with a loving mouth
Extend your palate
Enjoy all
Feel with loving arms
The smooth and the prickly
All that comes from not love
Has a reason
And it will at some time
In the presence and encouragement of love
Move towards that love
When it is ready
And not before

Boundaries

True love has no boundaries
and cannot be hurt

But if you would have boundaries
Let them be clear
And shine bright
and loving
Until they are ready to be dissolved
And all can be loved
without pain
For pain is a holding back
A holding back of love
A holding on, in fear, to what is
When you let go
Really let go
All boundaries will perish
And all will be one
One in love
In the One Heart

Irritation

I do not want to write today
I am irritated
And everything hurts
But the voice
The energy of love

Is still there
It urges me on
At first I am even more irritated
But I know
I feel
As I relax into it
All is well
My irritation is fine
It will come to pass
And love supports me
Until that time
Is come
And all is well again

Saints and sinners

How can you understand what it is
to be in the One Heart
Where all is one in love
Where there is no difference between
sinner and saint
Who amongst you has not had
a murderous thought
Men and women who murder

put into action
your thoughts as deeds
So that you can see them
and decide what you will do
or not do about them
Who amongst you has not had
one thought of altruism,
of inspiration and charity
Your Saints are those who put these thoughts
into action
so that you can see them
and decide what you will do
or not do about them
Sinners and Saints
You imprison one
And put the other on a pedestal
It is time to take responsibility yourself
For it all
And love it
In the One Heart

The Flame

No one is completely without love
In love we were created
And we will die into love
Whether we believe it
or act on it or not
It is the only way
The only reality
However hard we try to push love away
A spark will remain
Waiting for us to be ready
to ignite again
The flame of true love
Born out of the ashes
of disaster, hate or shame
It is the same in this world
and the next
Whenever we are ready
To believe in love again

Knowing

May you know what it is
To know my love
May you know what it is
To be my love
May you know what it is
To enact my love
May you know love
Love, love, love
Now and always
And be blessed
And you will know
In the fullness of time
Into the no time
What it is
To know fully
The One Heart
The One Heart
The rejoicing heart
The universal heart
of all that is
The One Heart
the golden heart
is a collective heart
ascended into a new dimension
A dimension beyond duality
beyond love and hate

and all the polarities
which bind us into
time on a linear scale
Love in the One Heart
is circular, timeless
It is without comparisons
It is beyond them
What does it feel like
It is beyond words
explanations
It can be experienced
when we go into the timeless zones,
in our dreams, our meditations
and sometimes our *real* lives
here on earth
It floods our very beings
Then we can feel safe
when we no longer need to feel safe
Flow and go
Into the light of love

Melody

Many are the days
When the light within you plays
a song of remembrance
of who you are
Who you really are
Which is love
But do you hear
or know
or act
on this
This being of light and love
within
Your true self
As you read these words
You will hear your song
more and more
Stop and listen now
Relax
into the tune
The beautiful melody
Feel it
Enjoy
Love to love and be love

At One

When you think of me
Be at ease with your thinking
When you feel me close
Be at rest with your feeling
When you know I am there
Be graceful with your knowing
When you hear me sing
Be harmonious with your hearing
When you speak of me
Be gentle with your speaking
When I touch you
Be the tenderness of my touch
When my love is there
Be at one with your loving

Return to Love

Thank you, dear sweet one
For letting me in
There is no place
In Heaven or Earth
Where I am not

And when you put yourself in hell
And close yourself off from me
I am waiting, patiently
For your return
To love

Tomorrow

Tomorrow is another day
when you can find love again
and forget all that has gone before
which has caused you pain
Start each day anew
with love as your focus
your reason for being
It will stand you in good stead
for all the ups and downs of life
And bring you
slowly but surely
to a safe harbour
Home
To love

Whatever

In the One Heart
is the acknowledgement
the responsibility
the knowing
at a very deep level
that we are all one
There is no you and me
just parts of me
Everywhere
in everyone and everything
making up the whole
The One
This is not just an abstract idea
It is a truth
A reality
And must be lived as such
What does this mean
It means whatever
you take it to mean
We leave it at that

Another, Yourself

Whenever you hurt another
You are hurting part of yourself
For we are all one
All is one
Whenever you criticize or defile another
You criticise and defile yourself
For we are all one
All is one
Whenever you love another
You are loving yourself
For we are all one
All is one
In the One Heart

Everything

Include in your One Heartedness
Not just all of humanity
But all the animals, plants
and all of nature herself
They are just as much part of you
Include also the angels

guides and masters
The unicorns, the crystals
The spirit within all
Include the whole universe
and beyond
The earth
The planets and stars
Even all the inanimate things
Include everything
All that is
In the One Heart

No Separation

In reality there is no separation
Separation is part of the
duality in this world
It does not necessarily
exist elsewhere
Can you get your head round this
Can you get your heart round this
We believe you can
We believe in you
and trust

All will be well
All is one

Time

No more crying
No more tears
The time is coming
To let go of all fears
And love is letting go of fear
The time is now
The time is here
Believe it so
And it will be so
True love is just around the corner

A New Way

Melt together in your oneness
Separate from your aloneness
And you will find
so much more
than you bargained for
than you ever dreamed was possible
The One Heart
is huge
A huge concept
A huge reality
As big as everything that is
And more
So much more
Believe in it
Trust and let this guide you on
Move you
to a completely new
way of being
in the One Heart

Be Who You Are

If you are feeling angry
Be angry
State your piece
If you are feeling sad
Be sad
Let the tears flow
Whatever you feel
Which is seemingly negative
Allow it
So that you do not block
The ultimate
The inevitable
Flow of love

Healing the World

The Healing Power of Love
is beyond measure
As you read these words
Send out your love
to all the world
And as you join with all others

who are reading these words
and sending out their love
to all the world
A Healing Power of Love
beyond measure
Fills this world, completely
With Healing and Love

ॐ ॐ ॐ

Come Back to Love

Many times when you feel lost and lonely
I am here to guide you
For I am love
Many times when you have lost your way
And do not know which way to turn
I am here to help you
For I am love
Many times when you feel disorientated and sick
I am here to heal you
For I am love
Many times when you do not know who you are
I am here to tell you
For you are love also
This is the core of your being

Do not forget that
Then you too
Can guide, help and heal others
Who are not sure
And have lost themselves
By straying away, for a while
From Love

Sounds

Let the music of love
fill your soul
with such sounds
as you have never heard before
Sounds which heal, embrace
Bring succour and a knowing
A wisdom which says
We are one, you and I
We are one

Love is Love

In the wisdom of the one heart
Love has no meaning
other than love itself
Love has no reason
other than being itself
Love has no goal
other than finding itself
Love is love, is love, is love
Everlasting

Relax

Let love flow through you
Allow it to flow
Release all impediments in the way
Relax and let it flow
May it flow through you
more and more each day
And anchor the blue print
of the One Heart

The Key

More and more we tell you
Love is the answer
Love is the key
Acceptance of yourself
and others
your situation in life
whatever happens
and has happened
close to home
and the whole world over
Will lead you to
an understanding
a compassion
a love
In the One Heart

Follow Love

When love beckons you on
Follow it closely
Through the fields
of yellow white daisies

Blue skies and crimson sunsets
The softening hearts
and tender eyes
White beaches, sun kissed skin
and gentle sea lapped shores
Crimson leaves and shapely trees
Snow clad lofty mountains
Temples silent and sparkling fountains
Gurus and tinkling bells
Peace in all, all thoughts quietened
Cool detachment in pools of compassion
In oceans of sense flooding love

Day to Day

The ordinary life
is never ordinary
Just living day to day
can take great courage
Living consciously
takes it a step further
Be not out of step with yourself
By thinking you do not matter
Realise each one of you is needed

on this planet earth
We hold you very dear to our hearts
The One Heart

All

The one heart shines
in the bodies of the Adonis
the Virgin,
the Madonna
and the face of the Mona Lisa
The One Heart shines
in bodies with eyes
that cannot see
ears that cannot hear
lips that cannot speak
limbs that cannot walk
or are missing altogether
The One Heart shines
in bodies black, white
red and yellow
in bodies straight or twisted
Do not think that you are exempt

Life's Way

Use love as a meditation
A mantra
Into the peace beyond
Use love as an affirmation
of who you are
and where you belong
Use love as a melody
A sweet refrain
as you sing your song
Use love as your foot steps
Each step of the way
As you journey along
Life's way

Touching Love

An innocent child skipping along
Lovers holding hands
A virgin bride in white
An old man with his woman's face
in his hands
Can make us smile

Forget this cynical world
And touch love again

ॐ ॐ ॐ

Love is There

The starving child in Africa
The soldier who lost his leg
The mother with a dying child in her arms
The woman being raped
The prisoner in a lonely cell
awaiting being tortured
The cancer victim in pain
The lonely, recently divorced or bereaved
All these things are separate from love
Are abhorrent to love
Yet love is there
Waiting in the wings
Until the person is ready
to heal
to move on
to change a shattered life
for the better
In this world,
or the next

Appearances

Sometimes
What's seen on the surface
The mottled skin
and wrinkles
Or even a wart
with a hair in
The rounded shoulders
and bandy legs
The layer of fat
and wobble
Belie the beauty
and love
that dwell within
And sometimes
it's the other way round

All is Love

Love, loving, loved
Lover, love child
Love lorne
Love – in

I love, you love
He loves, she loves
They love
God loves

ॐ ॐ ॐ

sharing

Some people think
that love is like a cake
And if I have a piece
and you have a piece
Then there will be
no cake left
But love isn't like that
We can go on sharing
and sharing
And you can have all the love
And so can you
and you
and you
In the one heart
there are an infinite
number of cakes
That can be eaten

over and over
Without being sick

য় য় য়

Open and Closed

The One Heart
Is not open today
No it is always open, to the fullest
Today it is my heart
My small, split - off ego heart
That says
Not today
Maybe tomorrow
When I have rested
I will pull on my courage and fortitude again
To open wide
And join with the One Heart
The beautiful, loving, huge, benevolent
One Heart
Thank you

In Love

Love of the one heart
Is where I am
I love – love
I am in love with love
I hate is out
I love is in
It makes me feel – wonderful
Even though everything in me hurts
One heart, one heart
Help me please
To be with you
And share
That love
In the whole
Universe

Oneness

The One Heart, the One Heart, the One Heart
I love that mantra
But what does it mean

That all hearts are one
Wow
That makes for a big heart
And a lot of love
It is so
If we join our hearts together
And love from them all
Then anything can happen
Big love for all
So much love
It is so ... love

ॐ ॐ ॐ

Everlasting

The One Heart
Is in you, in me
in everyone
We just have to know it
believe in it
To activate it
and join with
LOVE
Love eternal and everlasting
always has been

and always will
In the now
Be the love you are
Which is the all encompassing
One Heart
And be for ever more
In love
With love
For love
Thank you

ॐ ॐ ॐ

The Light

A light shines in the One Heart
for all those who are troubled
and sore and in pain
If that includes you
And it will do
Then allow this light
to open up your own heart
to the healing power
of the love
of the One Heart
Do it now

Do it always
And you are blessed

༃ ༃ ༃

Integration into Wholeness

The One heart
Is not just a high minded
ideal of spirituality
It is a reality that must
be grounded
Here on earth
To do this we must recognise
the split off parts of ourselves
Which we have banished in fear
The wounded heart
The abandoned and abused child
And integrate them into our
wholeness
With love and understanding
Alongside our expressions of
grief, anguish and anger
So that, through this long
and somewhat arduous process
An alchemy takes place

Transmutation, transformation
To a new place of wholeness
The One Heart

🜍 🜍 🜍

Carried by Love

When love no longer holds our hand
Or so it seems
We stumble and fall
in darkness deep
When love reaches in
uncovers our eyes
and carries us tenderly
We find strength
when we are ready
to reach out once more
To love
To wrap our arms
round Love's dear heart
And be at peace again

You Can

You can do it, you can do it
said love
No, I can't
Yes you can, you can do it
How
With all of my help, my love
You can do it
and do it well
Maybe
Just try, you can do it
I am here
I'll do it
I love you, you can do it
Thank you
It's done

Just as you Are

I am love
I see the perfection in who you are
Even when you feel you have failed
or that you are a failure
For me there is no judgement
You are perfect as you are
I am not referring to your potential
To what you could be
I am saying that you
are perfect as you are
Warts and all
For only when you can
feel this acceptance
And accept yourself as you are
Can you move and
expand into more
of who you are
And your true potential
Which is love

Comfort

I am honey to your mind
And chocolate to your soul
I am sunny skies
to caress your body
I am nectar to your heart
And I am a cool breeze to
your spirit
I am your strength to
carry on
And a cool glade to
rest in
I am warmth when you
are cold
And a soft bed to
lie on
I comfort you in
every way
If and when
you let me

Pain

Relax into your pain
whatever it is
Really go into it
Explore it
feel it
understand it
Do not fear it
At first it may appear
to get even worse
Until you come through
and it is gone

Push away your pain
Tell it
No
No more
I will not accept this pain
Until it is gone
Do whatever is appropriate
for you at the time
And come to love

How

How will I know you
Will it be by your scent
My scent is sweet, familiar, fragrant, nostalgic
How will I know you
Are you in what I see
I can be seen in everything
in everybody
in you
How will I hear you
You will hear my call
I speak in many voices
in all languages and tongues
in the wind, the sea
all nature
I am the hum of the universe
How will I know you
Can I touch you
Touch others and you touch me
How will I know you best
By presence and by my absence

Just Be

When you realise
that everything
that exists
is a part of you
in love together
Then you will know
The One Heart
When you go beyond words
and just be it
Then you have come home

Strength

The love of the One Heart
of compassion and understanding
Is not always soft and yielding
It takes a particular kind of strength
to love those others
or other parts of you
that hate you
It is easier to take your guns
your slings and arrows

Than it is to stay loving
in the harshest conditions
This does not involve
condoning or allowing
abuse
It involves staying still
in the One Heart
and transmuting alchemically
all that is not true love

STORIES OF LIFE, LOVE AND BEYOND

Stories you may relate to or find in others

and the tapestry of life and love

on earth and beyond

Dark Before the Dawn

I sit on my bed
Feeling empty
Drained
Tears only just
held back
Why, I have had this feeling
so many times
I am almost bored by it
And yet
it is this very place
which is always a prelude
to my greatest
inspirations
understanding
and love
So why hold back any longer
Let the tears flood
Let me be washed clean again
And live
Truly live

What is This One Heart

Many have asked me
When awake
And in my dreams
What is this One Heart
you talk about
What do you know about it.
I don't know anything about it
But I do know it

And so can you

Where All is One

As if in a dream
I awoke in The One Heart
It was quite dark
And yet everything sparkled
like the morning dew
My friends were all there
And also my enemies
Everything was new
Reborn

I asked
Where am I
The response came loud and clear
You are in a place
where all are one
Where there is no difference
between the sinner and the saint
Where each one
who is part of The One
Has no claim
to being better or worse
higher or lower
And at the same time
Individuality
That ability to be unique and different
is stronger than before
Here
there is no knowing
that has not always been known
No loving
that has not already been loved

The Scream

She was out in the countryside
Taking the dog for a walk
when she heard a scream
A very loud scream
from somewhere quite close
She looked around
But no one was there
Then she saw the tree
It was the tree that screamed
It looked like it had been struck by lightning
from its burns and scars
No it said
Two boys set me on fire
in the hollow in my trunk
The tree was devastated
aghast and horror struck
That humans could do such a thing
So she put her arms around the tree
And sent it healing thoughts
And love

A Way of Life

Many years ago, she can't remember
exactly when
She started on a journey
Which was to lead her
through many ups and downs
twists and turns
To Love
She was tired sometimes
on the journey
At other times despaired and alone
But she never gave up
Although sometimes she almost did
But now, making the journey
is a way of life
She wouldn't do it differently
And is glad
she started the journey
A journey of Love

Healing Abuse

She asked for love
And got a punch in the face
She asked for love
And got a mouthful of abuse
It took her a long time to realise
This was not love
Because in her childhood
It was the same
But when she did realise
She said No
And she started to learn
What love was
And gave it to herself
And asked people for help
Who knew how to give love
And love grew
And she gave it to others
who knew only abuse
When will the world be free
of all this mess
When it is ready
When all are ready
To say no to it
And discover what
real love is

Crying Out for Love

When you want to leave the planet
and everything you hold dear
When it all seems too much to bear
and you encircle a seemingly bottomless pit
and pain is all around
Then this is the time
to remember
to cry out
to shout
With all the force you can muster
No!
Love is here
Even though I no longer
see or hear it
Even though it seems way beyond my grasp
And if I hold this thought
tenuously at first
and then stronger and stronger
Maybe I can cry out for help
to love alone
or love in another or others
Then love will respond
Something will happen
an insight
a thought
an idea

a knowing
a helping
a shift in circumstance
a light breeze of hope
a sharing and a caring
And fingernails are carefully prised
away from the cliff to which they cling
And another pathway opens
another vista
another view
The tide has turned
and love is on
the horizon again
And love beckons forth
towards a new day

The Essene

When I was born into a life as an Essene
I was welcomed
by the community
singing my song
A song of life and love
I heard it always

when I needed it
or when I was really happy
Except when
the dark clouds gathered
and pushed it away
And once when I was travelling
out in the universe
I heard my note
A note of love
Like the song
it reverberated
through every part of
my being
Resonating
love with love
So that my whole being
expanded
in love
and in ecstasy
And we sang together
In love
Love has a sound
a note
a song
For each one of you
When you find it
We can sing together
In the One Heart

Daughter

Leo daughter
Laughing, sunny
Drama Queen
Leo rules the heart
they say
Sweetheart
My heart and yours
Forever

My Love

You taught me love
Like no one could
The hard way
and the easy
Husband mine
come very near
We're in this love
Together

She

She came to him in the morning
And stroked his brow
caressed his body
and gently ruffled the hair
on the crown of his head
But he did not allow her to stay for long
He had to put on his suit
his frown, his suit of armour
And in a controlled manner
go out to work
to fight
to prove himself
He had walled himself up
from the strength of her gentleness
So she lay dormant
deep within him

The Chase

I remember once
as I sat in the silence
Being an antelope

chased by a lion
There was no fear really
Just a feeling of energy
Of running away
As the lion pounced
Killed and devoured my body
It might have been horrible
for a person to watch
But for me
As the lion pounced
My spirit released
And all was peace
And quiet love

The Dream

It's only a dream they said
Only a dream
But to the child who had awakened
In fear and wonder
It was more
than a dream
It was a reality
that changed her

completely
And her understanding
of love
And anyway
What is real
And what is a dream
And does it matter anyway

ॐ ॐ ॐ

Together

Today
the one heart eludes me
eludes him
eludes us both
I reach inwards to find it
But first we have to express
our anger, our grief, our hopelessness
Release it, let go
What will happen next
we do not know
We just have to trust
the One Heart
within and without
and draw on the strength

the power
of love that knows no bounds
Trust is the essence
Fulfilling ourselves in love does not always come easily
It needs work and courage
Facing the reality of ourselves
enables us to move towards greatness
And the greatest of all
is love
in the One Heart
Together again in love
for love
Love always
in the now

Far Out

Far out into the universe I travelled
Past stars and planets
Into black holes and other universes
When I returned
I tried to put the experience
into words
that others could understand

It took time
There were blocks, critical,
jealous, fearful, are you crazy!
From without and within
But I held on to the experience
and what it really meant
at a deeper level
I really understood
whether others, or parts of me
liked it or not
And sometime later
I would find it in a book
or a TV programme
Being explained in a way that
put together
other people's explanation
In physical ways and the ways of physics
with mine
It helped
But mostly
On some deeper inner level
the experiences were there
as part of me
and who I am
And as ever
What held it all together
Was love
which never left me

or deserted me
however way out I went
And helped to integrate
my journeys
on all levels
I do not know how
But it did

ॐ ॐ ॐ

The Light of Love

Many people came to see her
For she radiated a certain light
Which attracted them like moths
to a flame
The name of the flame
was love, pure love
And they loved her for it
And she loved them
It rubbed off on them
Like touching the lamp of a genie
And the light of her love
ignited a spark within them
And they became a flame
A flame of pure love

And many came to see them
And so it went on
and on and on
Creating pure love
Everywhere

ॐ ॐ ॐ

The Madman

Love shows itself in
different ways
And people are not always
the way they seem
They said he was mad
He walked with a shuffling, muffling gate
which occasionally exploded into wild
rhythmic movements of ecstasy
Followed by
calm repose and slumber
He walked through crowds and saw
colours
which other people could not see
Some people looked into his eyes and saw
a depth
a universe

they could not understand
Others avoided him
and he was thankful
He spoke a language of gibberish, of nonsense
He knew it had meaning
form
beauty
It came from -
He knew not where
From beyond
The children loved him
but their mothers called them away from him
Hid them under their skirts
and carried them off
Muttering
The children looked back in innocence
a faint feeling of yearning inside their bellies
They put him in a place with bars at the windows
and men in white coats
But the bars at the window did not imprison him
His world had no boundaries
no limits
He went there
alone
No one could follow him
Alone, that is, except for the beings in white robes of
light
Who were, perhaps, related to the

men in white coats
He had much to teach them
They did not know
They did not realise that they were learning
not by a word
or a touch
or a look
Just by his being there
And the spirit within them was moved
And grew

And after he was gone
At least they thought he was
They said ...

Son's Gap Year

She knew she had to let him go
A gap year
Travelling
She had to really let go
In her heart
So he could travel
unencumbered

by apron strings
Such a hard thing to do
For a mother
She took her crystal
to the counsellor
A huge green gem
her husband bought her
in the Lake District
She talked for an hour
Struggled
I want to do it
she said
It's not easy
Then just as it was time to go
The counsellor
looking at her watch
All right
She cried
And then let go
She felt the release
It was a relief
And just at that moment
A loud crack
and part of the crystal
Split off
and flew into the air
Thank you
she murmured

and felt at peace
and joy
for his opportunity
his journey
Love is letting go
sometimes
And yet
at the same time
she held him in her heart
Forever
The One Heart

Trapped

She was giving a talk
to a women's group
about crystals
She showed them
pink ones, clear ones
purple and green
bright ones,
cloudy ones
gems large and small
One particular crystal

had another
embedded inside
Trapped
When the talk was over a women came up to her
That crystal
she said
The one that is trapped
That's me
Together they held
the crystal
and each other
with love
It's OK, she said
And left

The Concert

I went to a concert
given by Shri Chimnoy
at the Albert Hall
As we entered
we each were given
a white flower
When we were all seated
He came onto the stage

A tiny, big man
He sat down, cross legged
on the floor
And meditated
for what seemed a long time
During that time
My tooth
which had never
ached before
Became terribly painful
Oh no, I thought
Not here, not now
I decided to go into the pain
It got worse, and worse
Until it became unbearable
Hang in there I thought
And then suddenly
I broke through
Into bliss
No more pain
and a wonderful feeling
of lightness and joy
I was amazed
I remember reading
that this sometimes happened
to prisoners
who were being tortured
I enjoyed the concert

Cancer

There was heaviness around my abdomen
In my colon
It was so heavy and dark
I asked its name
Cancer, it said
At first I felt fear
Then I asked love for help
I knew, don't ask me how
It was not yet manifest in my body
Just an energy around
So heavy and dark
And soon it would come in
to my body
No, I said
This is my body
You don't come in
You are not invited here
I said this many times
every day
for a few months
Then one day
It was gone
And love filled my abdomen
instead

I said to love
Thank you
You are welcome

Stories

My stories are not my stories
They are stories of the whole world
The One Heart
Your stories are not your stories
They are the stories of the whole world
The One Heart
There is a world
a wealth of experience
In the One Heart
To pull on
And to move beyond
the stories
Into a beingness
Of love

The Guide

A nun appeared to me
She was his guide, I knew
You have to get him to a doctor
I had no idea why
I told him
He blanched
I have a lump he said
He went to the doctor
In a few days
he was in hospital
The lump, the cancer
was taken away
It changed his life
his way of living
for the better
He helped other people
with lumps
and all manner of things
Some years later
A friend did a drawing
of his guide
A man in chain mail armour
But the face was
exactly the same as the nun I saw
Love is there to help us
On all levels

In many different guises
If we are aware
Love is there

The Invisible Friend

Our child had
an invisible friend
whose name was Julia
They talked together
and played
every day
I could not see Julia
but I knew she was there
I trusted
When our child grew up
For Christmas
Someone painted her guide
She unwrapped the present
and looked at it
Oh, she said
It's Julia
Julia's picture now
hangs in her room
And looks on
with love

Blinking

I was in pain
out of sorts and disgruntled
Go to your bedroom and meditate
love said
Do I have to
I grumbled
But of course I went
As I sat there
Hundreds of past lives
passed before my eyes
Easy ones, difficult ones
Lives large and small
What's this all about
I muttered crossly
Then I got it
Each life is but a blink of an eye
Put your life into perspective
In the vastness of time
of being
So I did
And I felt better

The Love Bond

With tears in her eyes
she left him
in a box by the hospital gates
And turned her face to the city streets
and her respectable family home
Her heart was broken quite in two
And she wept each lonely night
For the love bond she felt
with her baby boy
Seemed stronger than anything she knew

As the years rolled by
She wondered often
what had become of him
Was he doing well, who cared for him
And she prayed every night for her child
Each birthday she lit a candle
Alone by herself in her room
Whilst her new family busied themselves
With no idea of the secret she held

And many, many years later
A letter arrived in the post
I've done some research
And I think that you are my mother
Can we meet and speak to each other

A turmoil of emotion flooded her body
At first she was all of a dither
But the love bond she knew inside herself
Was stronger than any other

They met in a cafe on London Road
He shared with her all his feelings
His anger, his doubts and his yearning
His story too and all that had happened
So much to say on that incredulous day
And the love bond between them
started to show in a way

There were things to unfold, families to be told
And the going was not always easy
But at the end of her days
When she closed her eyes
And drifted away to heaven
She knew for sure that her son was all right
And the love bond would never be broken
The experience they'd had, not easy she knew
Was one they had both of them chosen
To balance events from previous lives
And make things all right between them

And when she returned to him in his sleep
With ethereal hands she touched him
She said *thank you so much* as her kiss touched his cheek

He stirred in his dreams and saw her face
And murmured *mother* into his pillow
Our love bond will never be broken

Out of Body

I sat in the bath
Drained and empty
I had had enough
No more
I no longer wanted
to be
I was finished with it all
And then suddenly
I was on the ceiling
Looking down
in amazement
at my perfectly still
Still sitting up
Body
My husband entered the bathroom
Put down the loo seat and sat on it
Looking at me
Knowing something was happening

But he did not know what
Then I was in the tunnel
The long, dark tunnel
Whizzing down it
at a terrific speed
At the end was a light
So bright I could barely
bear to see it
So loving
So full of compassion forgiveness, understanding
Love
It changed me for ever
And yet
at the time
I was halted
Somewhere over my left shoulder
A voice, I think it was me
Said
You have to go back and face it all
So true
I knew it was true
In a flash
I was back
In the bath
But my body would not move
I panicked briefly
Then I said
Put your hand out and reach for the soap

My voice was slurred
As if I was drunk
But my body obeyed
I touched the soap
And gradually
I came back
And over the years
A changed and changing woman
I faced it all
With the help of the unconditional love
I experienced
at the end of the tunnel
At first I told no one
Near deaths and out of bodies
Were not spoken of then
I was afraid
they would think I was mad
But who is mad
The one in fear
or the one in love
I'm OK now
And thankful
To be
Here
In love

Love Never Ends

His mother lay dying
He knew not what to do
She was the centre of his universe
His source of succour too
He lay down beside her
Held her in his arms
I'm coming with you
She stared at him, alarmed
My son I'll be with you
For ever and a day
My love will never fail you
Even though my bones decay
My love will surround you
For you I'll always care
My love is in and around you
It's part of who you are
Care for your daughter
As I have cared for you
Pass it on, pass it on
Through each generation
And out through the nation
Into the whole world
And the universe beyond
Her eyes closed
She breathed her last breath
And surrendered into death

A loud wail rose from his lips
He knew not what to do
'Til a blanket of peace
surrounded him
She was gone, but was here too
Her love felt stronger than before
In waves it came, more and more
He saw her smile and wave
As if arising from her grave
A new man was born
No longer forlorn
But understanding
in a way quite quizzical
Of powers strong beyond the physical
He never knew before
And that love has no barriers
of time or place or form
It goes on forever
From mother to son
And on and on

To Grandad

The whistle sounded
and over the top they went
Into a battle of confusion
terror, wounding and death
His friend from the village
was at his side
His life long, true friend
A soldier ran towards them
bayonet in hand
And suddenly his friend was on the ground
Screaming
His eye pierced
with cruel steel
His gun in hand
the shot rang out
His friend was now at peace
But ever afterwards peace eluded his heart
What kind of man shoots his friend
Even to end his pain
What god is there in this rotten war
And yet, in truth, love was there
He helped his friend
What confusion in the heart
With turmoil still suppressed
Which went for his grand daughters' eye
In a moment

of defencelessness
with a cork screw
Grandad, I understand
I know what it cost you
I am not afraid
And I love you
And I thank you
for showing me
a tapestry of life
unfolding
And moving from hate
to forgiveness
From war into peace
And for returning
from the grave
to say sorry
All is love and love is all

Greater Love

She was growing old
and not well
Things were not as easy
as they had been

But slower
more painful
And she could not walk up the hill
to the shops there
But many came to visit
Not because she was old
or not well
But because she had a light inside of her
She told funny stories
which had them in stitches
and she cared about them
and loved them all
Which helped them
a lot
And when she died
and her children planned her funeral
as she would have wished
They came in their hundreds
Some silent
some in tears
They still felt her love
She was there
even though she was not there
Her love was greater
than an old, broken body
And it held them all

Possible Impossibilities

How do we love
When our daughter is raped
Or our son murdered
And our soul is on fire
We cannot
And yet
How can we not love
Eventually
Because only love will get us out of this mess

I was not sure whether to include this.

However I am mindful of Gandhi, who had to stop eating sugar himself before he could tell a child, whose mother had requested him to do so, to stop eating sugar/sweets.

Like many of you, I have suffered seemingly appalling tragedies in my own life, and with the help of love, come through. Not without scars and memories, but with increased courage, compassion and understanding.

It did not seem as if it would be possible, many times. Yet love took me by the hand; and eventually it was possible.

Love continues to lead me, however bleak life is at times.

And I am ever grateful.

Yet each time I sink into the pit, and for a time, forget love and suffer more, I discover again that love is patient and love is kind.

Then my gratitude grows, and love grows.

MORE MESSAGES OF LOVE

*Longer messages conveying the deeper meanings
of the love and the not love, providing insights as well
as reminders of all you really know and all you can be
in The One Heart.*

Because I Am Love

The One Heart
beats to the pulse
of the whole world
and beyond
It has a rhythm, a life which
is created
by you
By each one of you
from your own heart
Which may be
broken or whole
mended or in pieces
large or small
conscious or unconscious
divided and split
healed and renewed
dark or light
loving or hating
conditional or unconditional
Need we continue
You know your own heart
even when you think you do not
You see its reflection in the stars
the trees and fields
the seas and mountains
the bottomless pits

You have too long been divided
in your hearts
For many it continues
For some there is the glimmering
the knowing of how it would be
if all hearts were one

If all hearts were one
there would be no division
no suffering
no me against you
no conflict
no wars
You know this and yet
you continue to think unloving thoughts
Even though they may be quite subtle
for some of you
Why do I say this
To judge, punish and condemn
No, of course not
It is because I AM LOVE
That I say these things
It is because I AM LOVE

A Truth

The One Heart
Sometimes I think it is an illusion
Created by my own poor, needy mind
At other times
I am aware of it as
an inspiration
a motivation
towards something good
But that doesn't feel right either
It's not true
What is true
What I feel to be true
In my very bones
In every part of my being
Is that it is a truth
As yet not fully uncovered
or understood
But it is there
Waiting for us to develop
the ability
to comprehend it
Once and for all
And then to live it
So that we become true
To ourselves
To everything

To Love
To the One Heart

ॐ ॐ ॐ

The Message

When you write these words
of the One Heart
There is part of you which
is concerned
they are airy fairy
and will be judged
to be without substance
And yet in the very fact
that you write them
They are grounded in reality
Not just with the paper and pens
But in the fact that they are
relayed to you
From your deepest knowing
to your conscious mind
Which can then understand them
use them
Convey them
to the larger mind

of the world
in your reality
As you say them
to just a few
or many
As others read them
The real message of love
is conveyed to all hearts
And together
as the One Heart
You can change the world
As your understanding of
love
The poetry and the
reality of love
Becomes
truly grounded
by all
and spreads
Not just its message
But its Beingness
And its Beingness in Action
All is well my dear
All is well

Destiny

To know the One Heart
is to love eternally
For how else would love be
To try to separate it
into small parts
into time
To analyse it
To call it this and that
Is an endeavour
which will never give
the full understanding
and experience of love
Do not despair that
there is far to go
You are closer than you think
dear ones
For in your dreams, sleeps
and meditations
You are being contacted
by beings of love
Who shine
their radiance
forth
So that you may understand
In some measure
What is your ultimate destiny

You are more than you think
You are love

ॐ ॐ ॐ

I Will Light Your Way

I am love
If you allow me to permeate every part of your being
I will wash away all pain
I will support you in whatever
it is
you have to do
or want to do
I am here for you always
And when you begin to understand
to comprehend
what I am
Love perfected
Then you will begin to see your life
begin to change
In all ways
in seemingly miraculous ways
in ways you would not have
thought possible
You will see yourself

and the world
through different eyes
You will be surprised at what you find you know
Without even trying
you will start a new life
in a new world
The world of the One Heart
Be at peace and allow
all to come to you
As you allow the flow of love
through you
now and always
Though your heart is not strong
With me it is strong
Although you are not willing
With me there is
all the willingness in the world
Though your feet walk not on the path
I am the way
and the footsteps
in which your feet can walk
Although you walk in the shadows
I will light your way, I am your all
I am everything you need
When you come to me in distress
I will calm you
When you feel alone
I will be with you

When you understand not
who you are
why you are here
and where you are going
I will light your way
For I am love everlasting
I provide a coherence of energy
within your soul
When you know love
You know yourself
and others
and the world
Your purpose becomes clear
And there is nothing you
do not understand
There is no need really
to understand
Just be with me
I am all you need
to be free
of all doubts and fears
And go with the flow
The flow of love everlasting

Eternity

I will be with you always
Do you know what that means
Always is an awfully long time
Quite beyond the comprehension
of the limited mind
the dualistic mind
To comprehend always
what it means
in the no time
the circular time
whatever you call it
You need to surrender your mind
to me
And acknowledge that beyond words
beyond time
Is the knowing
The knowing of what it means
to love and be loved
in eternity
So surrender now
if you wish
By just being willing
And asking and praying
And let the understanding
the comprehension
Come, like a gentle breeze

And bathe yourself in the understanding
of your soul
And me

❦ ❦ ❦

The Lighthouse

Like a lighthouse
I stand on the rocks
of your destruction
or seeming destruction
at times
of yourself
and of the world
Like a lighthouse
I beam out a signal
of hope
for those who can see
Like a lighthouse
I am steadfast
and can never be extinguished
I am your light
your life
your world
Allow me to be ignited

in your heart
in every part of your being
Then you too
can be a light in the world
A way shower
A person no longer in the shadows
of your own weakness
and ignorance
But strong in your knowing
and seeing
That all is not lost
It never is
My light can never be put out
And nor can yours
The name of the light is love
and there are many other aspects
and qualities
attributed to the light
For the light in the lighthouse
has many facets
and it turns
through three hundred and sixty degrees
A complete circle
Never ending cycles that come
and go
but never stop
Be of good cheer
Never fear

My light is with you
Always

ॐ ॐ ॐ

Beginnings and Endings

Where shall we begin
to tell you the power of love
and the loveliness of love
everlasting
For in reality there is no beginning
and no end
Yet you desire your beginnings and endings
So you can see how far
you have travelled
And where you have come from
and gone to
This is all very admirable
And part of your experience
in duality
Where you can learn more
about yourselves
and who you are
And take back this growth
in maturity

To your soul
Where you already know
who you are
It can all seem so complicated
and un-necessary
at times
But you have chosen
this experience
All of you together
Because it does
have value
And in a way
Adds a totally new
dimension
To who you are
Many of you are in service
in this world
Which will complement
who you are
Many of you are bringing
the light of true love
to this world
Which will intensify the flame
of who you are
Some of you seek nothing
in this world
I say to you all
You are doing fine

Here in this world
Enjoy it
Stay and enjoy
Being who you are
Now and Always
In Love

ॐ ॐ ॐ

Forgiveness

How is it
That beyond forgiveness
There is no need for forgiveness
This is because forgiveness
brings love
compassion and understanding
that nothing is wrong
In the One Heart
there is no right
or wrong
Only love
Love understands that so called wrong doings
come from feelings of hurt and pain and revenge
When we are hurt, abandoned, abused
We will take the feelings that stem from these

and turn them in on ourselves,
causing ourselves pain and illness
Or we will turn them outwards
towards other people
Until we become conscious
of what we are doing
And start to change it
to move through the pain towards love
The not love feelings
and the patterns and ways in which they are expressed
may come from the present
from childhood
from ancestors or genes
from past lives
from thoughts of the future
from Karma and more
Make no mistake
There is no condoning of misdemeanours
large and small
But through understanding and compassion
There can be a balancing
A return to the fulcrum
of love
When we hurt another, we hurt ourselves
When we hurt ourselves, we hurt another
This is the way it is
Do we have to forgive the way it is
Or accept it and move on

to show this is not the way it is
In the new way that it is
In the One Heart
there is no separation
no pain
no need for retribution
Only acceptance and love for all
Do we need to forgive Love

The Helpers

Many are the ones who will assist you
in these coming times
Many are the ones who wait patiently
for you
to open your hearts
to become the One Heart
Many are the ones who will give you love perfected
Every moment of your life
Day and night
Do not despair dear ones
When things do not appear to be going as well
as you think they ought
or would like them to be

We are assisting you in more ways
than you know
Allow these words to gladden your heart
To lift you up
into the light of lights
the love of all
in the One Heart
We thank you too
For your efforts, patience and persistence
You are indeed
Workers of the light
and love
of the One
And we are grateful

Beyond Pain

When in your pain
you groan and moan
and cry out for help
Have faith
and love
and understanding
And trust that your cry

will be heard
Will shatter the pain
and fill the spaces with love instead
Will bring you knowing
of all you need to understand
and do or not do
to root out the cause and source
of your pain
Will help you to let go of resistance
to your pain
to relax into it
to let go
To love even pain
as part of your journey and path
towards wholeness
To speak to it
image it
know and understand it
and the message it has for you
And to help others in their pain too
We know that this will help you
for this is love in action
And your cries are heard
for we love you

The Wholeness Beyond Safety

There are some who feel safest on earth
And dismiss ideas of the spiritual
Of other dimensions
and beings of light
and more
as fantasy
because they fear it
Until in some way they are
awakened
broken open
And become aware
whilst still staying rooted
There are others who feel the safest in
other worldly realms
And resist
being grounded and solid
on earth
which they fear
Until they too are awakened
Helped to face their fears
and become grounded
There are some who feel safest in the
world of intellect and ideas
and clever arguments
Until they are awakened
to feel and know more

The reality of things
in heaven and on earth
There are those who feel safest in the
drama of their feelings
and let it all hang out
Until they are awakened
To find the peace within
And beyond
And as all become more whole in themselves
No longer dismissing others as crazy or unenlightened
They can meet and understand
each other
In wholeness
In reality
As one, loving heart

Trust

How can you trust love
How can you not
You have trusted what you call love
But which was not love in reality
Love which was instead
your crying out for love

your neediness
your fantasy
your co-dependence
your trying to fill the gap
of where you have known not love
Your lack of love for yourself
has led you into alleyways
of darkness, pity
and despair
And you have said
I no longer trust love
But you do not know what love is
The love, the love of which I speak
Will never let you down
Will be there through
rainy days and sunny days
Will support you
Will always want what is best
for you
And yet the love of which
I speak
Is so much more than this
Is so much more than you can
ever imagine
How can you know
what you have never known
How can you feel
what you have never felt

By asking of course
Ask and ask and ask
And stay open for the reply
the experience
of this love of which I speak
See with your eyes
See love everywhere
Even in the darkest places
It is there
Waiting.
Being
Open your eyes and see
It is in you
Feel it
Know it
And if you cannot
Be willing
Be willing to open your self
And know love
Everywhere
All of humanity has struggled
far and long
with these issues
of love
Of knowing a loving God
rather than a God of war and hate
Of knowing and expressing
the love within

A few have done this
You call them saints, prophets, gurus
and even God
Now is the time for everyone
Yes, I mean everyone
To open to love
To know love
As it really is
I can not explain it to you in words
There are no words
with which to express it
But I can help you to know it
If you really ask
If you are really willing
I need to know you are
committed
Really committed
To knowing love
It is only by commitment
That anything is achieved
Otherwise the result is half-hearted
Wishy-washy
If you really want love
Then say so now
And I will hear
And help you clear the way
Clear your path
Which is strewn with boulders

of doubt, of mistrust
Do not berate yourself
for this
Love yourself as I do
now and always
And then sweep your way
clean and clear
And come to me
I am waiting
And when the time is right
I will run forward to greet you
And hold you in my arms
And lay my lips on yours
I am love
Love everlasting
Undiluted
Perfect
Brilliant
Radiant
True
Be brave dear one
and take your chance
LET GO AND LET LOVE

The Eyes of Love

The eyes of love
are deep pools of compassion
and understanding
They shine with a brilliance
almost too bright to bear
They encompass you completely
unconditionally
They are so
beyond what is known
That you sometimes turn away
In awe, in fear
But then look back for a few
seconds
And a few seconds more
and more
As gradually you allow them
to embrace you
You allow yourself to begin
to understand
what they say
You let them melt you
And the molten you
is moulded into a different form
You begin to recognise yourself in them
And look and see
with loving eyes

Yourself
And as the eyes of the world
Become loving eyes
They see a new world
And a new world of love
is created
and becomes a reality
A loving eye for a loving eye
Makes the whole world
Love

On Your Way Home

On your way home
Do not forget those who have helped you
Given you a helping hand
A map, a route
A bridge to cross over
And even a mountain to climb
There are those who have been caring and sharing
Full of wisdom
wise words and faith
There are those who have put you down
and done you in

Who also helped you become strong for the journey
But most of all
There is the beacon
the light of love
Which has shone brightly
And pulled you on
through dark days and bright days
Moreover, there is the journey itself
And when you have arrived at your destination
Or at least you think you have
Let the newly distant hills
beckon you on
For you are growing
In your journey
Becoming always
More than you are
Resting on the journey
at times
On your way home
To love

Do Not Despair

Do not despair little one
For when you fall into despair and hope eludes you
You lose sight of the wonderful future
that lies ahead of you
As you continue to be open
even when times seem hard
We are able to contact you
be with you
and show you the way back to love
But we need your permission
Your openness
Your yay, not nay
Without this we are not able to do anything
to help you change your situation
We want to help you
We very much want to help you
We would like to take you by the hand
So to speak
And show you that there is no need for regret
No need for pain and tension
No need to resist what is
These seeming needs are the needs of the mind
which dwells in the duality of good and bad
And seeks to think, to figure out how to be happy
again
But happiness cannot be figured out

In trying to think a way out
you may convince yourself all is well for a while
But the mind goes round in circles
and you are back where you started again
With our love you may still be up and down at times
But there will be sense of direction
of knowing
of fulfilment
In finding, not only the way
but a sense of self
a sense of who you are
Which is love
And love guides you on
and seeks nothing but itself
It has been there since time immemorial
and it continues to be so
For to love is to love
This is your way out of your despair
And in doing this
In the One Heart
You are doing it
not just for yourself
but also for all the others
who despair
and have lost the way
Be a way shower
for the way of love

When Love is First

Put love first
In all that you do
If you are making money
do it with love
and for love
If you paint a picture
paint it with love
If you go for a walk
walk with love
and see the love
all around you
Put love in your work
and work with love
Love your body
in sickness
and in health
And in your relationships
Put not yourself first
or the other
Let love be the focus
If love is first
and foremost
All else will follow
harmoniously
beautifully
Put love first

in your meditations
your affirmations
your unconscious mind
and your spirit
And put love first
consciously
with consciousness
If love is first
your life will flow
Will help you and others
Will be a worthwhile
and fulfilling
life to have lived
When love is first

self Forgiveness

Why is it so difficult to forgive ourselves
Usually even more difficult in the end
than forgiving others
Love yourself so that you can love others
they say
Is that more difficult too
And how did

love others as you would love yourself
Get translated into
love others more than yourself
Perhaps it's this
We know when others have hurt us
In a tangible way
But we don't know the inner
silent thoughts
They direct adversely
towards us
Yet we know ourselves
In all the inner
and outer ways
we transgress
We know, not only
our actions
but our thoughts
and feelings too
which need redemption
And another thing
We know the events
the cutting hurts
we need to forgive
in others
These things that have transpired
in a single moment
or more
or over the years

But with ourselves
we know the things we do
that we would rather not have done
or said,
or thought or felt
on a daily basis
So day by day
they build up
From day dot
until now
Wow, that's an awful lot of forgiving
Maybe we need to
do a bit of
self forgiving
or ask for it
every day
And perhaps, under the circumstances
We're doing quite well
And also we need to know
that love forgives
the big things
as well as the
many
every day
accumulated things
Well maybe then
We can forgive ourselves
And then there is the fact

That when we take on the responsibility
that we are all one
Then we are responsible
for everything
That's a lot to forgive
and to be forgiven for
But one by one
and together
We can do it
Because in the end
There is nothing
to forgive

Being and Doing

Love is both a noun
and a verb
It is a being and
a doing
Love in the One Heart
Is being in action
What does that mean
It means that as you love
you are love

And that as you are love
you show this in all that you do
for self and for others
and more
Being and doing love
It goes together
I am love
I do love
They go together
because just being is not always enough
What you are
your beingness
needs also to move
and to share
Love stands alone
And at the same time it moves
itself and others
and the world
To greater states of being
and doing, and being
Do you understand my dear
how the vastness of love
Is and moves and has its being
It is creation
at its most fundamental
It is experience
in its Highest Glory
It is so much more than you realise

You see the effects of love
in your charity
your giving
You feel it
in your most profound relationships
You hear it in the bird song
in nature
in your lover's voice
But do you know
there are sounds
visions, sensations
Beyond your wildest dreams
which come into manifestation
For those who hear celestial music
and translate it into musical composition
For those who see visions of light and love
and translate them into beautiful pictures
or sculptures or films
For those who dance
the dance of Life
For those who live what they sense
at higher or deeper levels
Beautiful but poor by comparison
There is so much more for you
to do and be
Be patient
Meditate
Ask

And all will be given
unto you
In time
The right time for you
As you touch the no time
The beingness
The doingness
Of love

ॐ ॐ ॐ

The Best is Yet to Come

The best is yet to come
As more and more of you
realise what it is to be
in your own heart
and the One Heart
The best is yet to come
as you allow yourself
to love more than you
have ever loved before
The best is yet to come
as you know me
Really know me
and know you are me

Love
The best is yet to come
as your consciousness expands
Clearing, not fearing
along the way
All that is in its way
'Til the purity of true love
shines forth
And creates, co-creates
a better world
For you and all that dwell
on and within the beingness
of your world
The best is yet to come
as you open yourself
to the golden rays
of the golden heart
of a New Golden Age

With My Love

No longer do you dwell in darkness
With my love
No longer are you poor in spirit

With my love
No longer do you thirst or hunger
or have nowhere to live
With my love
My love does not allow all that
But sometimes you allow it
When you have fallen out of love
with yourself
others
and the world
Reclaim my love for yourself
And all else will follow
Reclaim it by moving, being
asking, praying
affirming
Whatever methods appeal to you
But most of all
trust
Have faith in what you do
And in the way these things
come to pass
Do not say
I asked for this
and it did not come the way I expected
Do not stay for ever in the darkness
before the dawn
Instead, let my light
The light of love

Lead you on
Lead you on
Until you are with me again
in your fruition
The abundance
and fulfilment
Of everlasting love

ॐ ॐ ॐ

Learning to Walk with Love

There is nowhere I am not
I fill all the spaces
in your heart
in everything
I am the cement which joins things together
I am a necessary component
to make sense
of everything
When you shut me out
and feel depravity
despair
I may seem not to be there
But how can that be so
I am everywhere

The not love
is part of the love
In the One heart
Your smaller minds will not
be able to comprehend this
Your larger minds
and love
comprehend it all
You stand
and you fall
repeatedly
Until you learn to walk
and you learn to love
My love stays steadfast
in the face of all opposition
And so do you
believe it or not
How else are you still here
And you will always be
Wherever you are
You are indestructible
And so is love
Be at peace
Dear one
Be the love you are
Even in the presence of not love
Because love is where you are
and who you are

Now and always
For ever and ever
in love
with love
surrounded by love
Love
Let the word caress you
Be at peace

ॐ ॐ ॐ

A Vessel of Love

As the words flow through me
They speak of love
Will you allow yourself to know them
To let them flow
into every part of you
Mind, Body and Spirit
Now and for ever more
Be still my dear one
And know these words
of love
Let them transmute, transform you
Gently
So you become

a vessel of love
Seeking to be open and available
for all those
who come into contact with you
Who need the love
that you are
Be it
Be the One Heart
For I am very near
There is no me
There is no you
There is just
Love
Everlasting
Be free
And enjoy
all that love offers you
All that love is

Empathy

Empathy
That ability
to feel another's pain
as your own
Do that
and then
transmute it
into the love
Of the one heart

Empathy
To feel another's hate
as your own
Do that
and then forgive it
Into the One Heart

Empathy
To feel another's despair
Do that
and heal it
Into the One Heart

Empathy
To feel another's joy
as your own
Do that
and bring that also
Into the One Heart

Empathy
To feel another's peace
Do that
and bring it into
the One Heart

Empathy
To feel another's sense of oneness
Do that
and be
the One Heart

A Path

Forgive yourself
And forgive others
Keep on forgiving

and forgiving and forgiving
This a path
That will lead you to
The One Heart

Love yourself
And love others
And keep on loving
and loving and loving
This is a path
That will lead you to
The One Heart

Be kind to yourself
And be kind to others
And keep on being kind
and kind and kind
This is a path
That will lead you to
The One Heart

Have compassion for yourself
And have compassion for others
And keep on having compassion
and compassion and compassion
This is a path
That will lead to
The One Heart

Living in the Love

When you put pen to paper
and write these words
You do not know
what word will next appear
Because you write each word
as it comes
Not thinking what is next
Letting go of what is already written
This is the way you can lead your life
Living in the now is a popular concept
Although some say these words
without really knowing
what they mean
However we might call it
Living in the love
The timeless love
The love almighty
But what exactly does it mean
It means living each moment
With love at your centre
In your very being
Conscious of that fact
that you are love
And as you stay centred in love
in each moment that passes
You become someone

who acts as a beacon
A stabiliser
for all who are seeking love
Outside themselves
and within
You are no longer a seeker of love
You are a finder
a beingness of love
There are many who will
misunderstand you
And translate your way of being
in projections of the parts
they do not own within themselves
And think that that is who you are
Be not dismayed or swayed by this
Just allow them to be who they are
and who they are not
You will find
As you stay
more and more
in the centred space and place
of love
That you are able to love
and cope with
more and more
And then everything
that threatens to topple you
from a place which many desire

and many are afraid of
and many would prefer that others do the work
and imagine that they can themselves reap the rewards
Of course it does not happen this way
How does it happen
There are many ways
Probably as many as there are people
However a few guidelines might be
ask and ask and ask
and then ask some more
on a regular basis
Clear out from yourself all that
is not love
Sometimes an arduous process
although not always
Believe and trust
in yourself
and also in love
And do this with
a fervour and a desire
For nothing less
than your goal
of true love
The love of the One Heart
Know that you are being watched over
and helped
Even when you do not think or
feel you are

If it helps you, offer rituals
dances, celebrations and flowers
Also you can meditate and pray
Which of these paths is the greater,
the easier
It depends on each individual
Their path through this life
and the history etcetera they bring with them
But know most of all
You will all get there
Find it
In the long run
or the short one
There is no doubt about it
We are all going in the same direction
To Love Eternal
Even though the individual twists and turns
and alleyways
would seem to dictate otherwise
Because in reality
You are already there
You are eternal love
You just don't know it

A Diamond of Love

Sometimes love is gentle and kind
and transmutes the not love
As a soft cleansing rain
Sometimes love rages with a passion
And storms and hurricanes blaze through the not love
So that the whole being shivers and shakes
In awe of the splendour and might
Which devastates all that has
become obsolete
in the beingness of love
Love in the One Heart
is a multifaceted diamond
It shows itself in many ways
many colours, many hues
of sparkling energy
The diamond is hard
The compression of many layers
of a mineral which was
originally much softer
The result of many years
in the formation
In its finished form
it is a jewel of great beauty
Often given as a symbol
of the joining together
of two people

in love
As you become a diamond
of love
Honing every aspect of yourself
And your life
Polishing every facet
Let your beauty and your love
Shine
And adorn the whole world
with its splendour
and its glory
A tribute in love
to love
Forever

In The Air is Love

In the garden of the One Heart
There are flowers
the like of which
you have never seen before
With colours
so beguiling
you never knew existed

With perfume
overwhelming
carrying you off
into degrees
of rapture
There are trees which offer shelter
and talk to you
There are birds
you can follow
in your flight
into realms unknown
And wild animals
who pet you
and show you how
to be strong
There are crystals
bright and shining
healing
conveying love
and wisdom
never touched before
There are people
you have known
and not known
Who feel like home
and tell you
all you want
and need to know

and all you have known
There are libraries
full of books
where you can learn
all that is and all that has been
and all there will ever be
There are temples
of healing
which heal you into
your utter and complete
being of love
There are places for rest
and peace
and for dancing and fun
And tangible
pervading the air
is a profound sense
a depth of wisdom
a knowing that here
You and your creator are one
And you are created
and perfected by love
Yes, love is in the air
in the One Heart

Believe in Love Again

What do I write of the One Heart
I write that the One Heart
has served me
when I was alone, felt alone
And helped me to realise
that I am never alone
Love is always there
It never goes away
even when I do
I write that the One Heart
has enfolded me in love
when I was abandoned
and abused
And has helped me to be strong
and rebuild my life again
I write that the One Heart
has linked me to people
also of the One Heart
And we have shared together
much of great value
and beyond words
I write that the One Heart
has helped to make me whole again
when I have been crippled by pain
down and out
And has restored once more

my belief in love
I write that the One Heart
has been the cement in my life
in the broken places
The One Heart has taken me to places
I never before knew existed
And I have realised that we are all one
Co-creators in the One Heart
of a universe of Love
Now is the time to bring the understandings
of the One Heart
To Planet Earth
and all who dwell on and with her
Now is the time to take responsibility
for what we create in love
and to let go of all that has been created
in not love
For now is the time
more than ever before
to be in love with
God
Ourselves
The universe
And everything
And to give thanks

Knowing Love

When the fog has cleared from your vision
You will know love
When the cool breeze
clears out your lungs
You will know love
When the wind of change
blows through your veins and arteries
You will know love
When the iron clamp
releases your muscles
You will know love
When the fiery storm
unburdens your nerves and brain
You will know love
When the cool earth
softens your feet
You will know love
When the music of the skies
fills your ears
You will know love
When clouds of truth
fill your mouth and throat
and sweet nectar fills your stomach
You will know love
When the band of steel
falls from your heart

When the healing power of love
fills every nook and cranny
of your body and mind
You will know love

The One Time

Letting go is letting go of time
as you move into the one time
the light of the One Heart
My dad used to say, *How's the enemy*
when he was late and
running out of time
Time is not the enemy
But now is the time
to let go of time
Those of you who have consciously
dedicated yourselves
to the light
The light workers
will feel this more than most
As time recedes
Creating temporary stress
for the body mind
which doesn't like change

and letting go of the known
in order to move into the unknown
But your time will come
Your time of timelessness
In the now
In the One Heart
Be of good cheer and know
there are those that assist you
on every level
every second of time
To come to
to be with
The One Time

ॐ ॐ ॐ

The Way Shower

Are you a fairy or an elf or a gnome
Are you an angel or a star traveller
Changing form in this dimension
is not easy
Yet there are those who have created
and then uncreated
illness, tumours and other things
I remember the girl

With the head of thick, long, glossy
curly hair
I asked
Did you not lose it when you had the chemo
No, she said
I imagined the chemo making it
healthier than before
Imagination is the key
to creating heaven on earth
If we just believe
and put in the effort
consistently
What can we create together
for the betterment of all
And for those who have tried and failed
Nothing is ever lost or wasted
How many people tried to climb Everest
or make a car or a medicine
or run a four minute mile
Before someone did
Helped by the beliefs and efforts
of those who had gone before
And suddenly lots of
people could do it
and can do it
Perhaps you are a way shower
of what can be done
Even when you don't quite make it

Boundaries and Discernment

I once wrote
For everything I say to you
The opposite is also true
In a world of duality
Perhaps this is so
So when you read my words
Listen with discernment
What level are they coming from
And they come from many levels
What rings true for you and what does not
And this will be different for everyone
According to, not only their point of view
but also as a result of many different
paths
experiences
ideologies
genetics
karma
you name it
This does not weaken,
whatever is written
It merely allows for all the parts
all the people
that make up the whole
But be careful
If you view from a fragmented self

You will see merely fragmentation
contradictions, confusion, distortion
and so on
If you view from your whole, centred self
You will see through to the essence
in everything
In a way which is not merely understood
But knows
Really knows
What feels right
at the heart of things
beyond the seemingly split
seemingly paradoxical distortions
You will see all the things which can be held
together
In an ocean of truth
An important point to consider
in saying and hearing
Is where do the words come from
From love
or not love
And if we are really in touch with love
Those words which come from not love
can be allowed also
Although not necessarily condoned
Especially if they are put into action
The paradox is
that if we hold the not loving things

in love
they will eventually transmute
Because all they ever wanted
all along
Was to be loved
And in their not love
they tried to draw this to our attention
Like naughty children
who need boundaries
But also to be held
with love

ༀ ༀ ༀ

Changing

The One Heart flows
is not static
It moves and changes
with the times
Nothing is set in stone
The one heart is not set in stone
It moves and changes
Forever

Without change, there is no love
Without movement
There can be no understanding
of the ever changing universe
of the love of and in the universe
Love is an energy which adapts
to all changing circumstances
Evolution
Notice how the first four letters
spell the word
invoke the essence of
Love
Love is change, transformation
evolution
Love always and you will change
Transcend to ever expanding
ideas and understanding of
Love
For now be at peace
Be in love
And acknowledge the
ever changing, ever loving
YOU

Namaste

We, the One Heart, love everyone
who has been used
abused
Is in pain
illness
poverty
or lovelessness
And that includes
Everybody on earth at this time
Who has at some time
touched the darkness
and negativity
of this planet
Your fears and hopes are known
We now bring you a
healing
Through unconditional love
To all who read these words
Namaste
One more time we tell you
Love is all there is

A Time of Love

The One Heart is forever
It is, always has been, always will be
Ever since the beginning of time
When two humans lived here
on earth
At a human level we are often
divided
But at another level
All hearts are one
Are part of and at the same time
the whole of
The One Heart
It has always been so
In the past
this has been understood by the few
The time has come, is coming
When it can be understood
as well as felt
and known
By the many
This will be a time of rejoicing
A time of love
and peace on earth
As we return to
As well as become
The One Heart

Be at peace and know
that it is good
It is good

ॐ ॐ ॐ

Love asks Nothing

So many times
We close down
our hearts
and become separate
alone and afraid
Why
Because believe it or not
We are afraid
of the magnitude
of the great love
of what it can do
And also what it may ask
of us
It asks nothing
It is we who ask
the impossible
The impossible is how to
live

without the love
Be brave dear ones
And be
In love
Be the One Heart
you are

Experiencing Love

The one heart is BIG
It is bigger than you can ever imagine
Bigger than your wildest dreams
What is it you may ask
Does it have form, structure
Is it pure energy
In reality, what it is, matters not
It is only in your world of duality
You would have it pinned down
explained
scientifically valued
put on a board and dissected
We would that you have none of this
Think of it, if you like
as an energy

a metaphor
for your understanding
But in truth
It can only be felt
be experienced
And then you will have no doubt
what it is
How can I do that
you may ask
Feel it, experience it
Well, by being open to the idea of it
Surrendering everything in your life
you hold on to
Not just materially
by being willing to let go of everything
if asked
But also by walking, alone
naked and unfettered into
LOVE
This not an easy thing to do
But is not difficult also
If you, trust, ask, receive
have no expectations
And dedicate your beingness to
LOVE
We ask nothing of you
Yet we seem to ask everything
And that is also true

But do you not know
that you were meant to read this
at this time
Because you have some glimmering
or a smattering or a huge amount
of knowing
already
All we ask is that you
know what you know
You are love
You are the One Heart
already
You always have been
and always will
But now it is coming to fruition
to maturing
In the no – time
which approaches fast
Be not afraid
Be who you are
Look into my eyes
And know
where you have been
and where you are going
and where you are now
You have been in the One Heart
for eons
The One Heart does not fail you

But at times
you fail yourself
The One Heart says
That is OK
It is alright
It is fine
It is part of who you are
Here
But in the One Heart
you cannot fail
It is an impossibility
Come, love
Come

Love's Power

The Power of Love
exists in the One Heart
So no matter who you are
or where you are
or what you are
This Power exists in the One Heart
In your HEART centre
It is no use denying it

For one day it will burst forth
Disguised as pain release
tears
explosive negative emotions
Which lead you to
its truth
The truth is
You are scared of love
You want to pretend
you know what it is
That you are using it, living it, being it
with yourself and others
The truth is, there are not many
who truly know and use
the power of love
And for them, not all the time necessarily
But the time is coming
When the power of love
will change the world
One person at a time

You are Never Alone

Many are the times
in a person's life
on earth
when you lose heart

To lose heart is
to think
you are alone
In your aloneness
comes many fears
and doubts
Yet always
it is possible
to know
that if you ask for help
Really, really ask
and really mean it
Then the light of love
will come
Perhaps gradually at first
alongside the misgivings
and pauper attitudes
And then at last
coming slowly
or even in a quick
almost explosive
event or realisation
That shatters all former
knowing
Bringing new knowledge
That love is the answer
Love is the key
we have been looking for

And it is good
It holds out its hand
to escort us
on the long, long journey
Back home
to ourselves
Where we are no longer
Alone

Born to Love

And now Pam
Yes
We address you by name
Who are we
Who speak through you
We are love
you are connecting to
Coming from
The essence and particles of
love itself
Which is the glue that
holds together
The planets

The universes
All beings on all levels
that exist
everywhere
We are love, love, love
As you know it, will it
and have experienced it
Through all the times and all the ages
As love has grown and nurtured
Then diminished and almost
seemingly disappeared
And then burst forth again
In even more splendiferous ways
Do you not know
you were born to do this
As is everyone who so wishes
and is prepared
to look for love
ceaselessly
We wonder how you come to know
The love that continues to flow and flow
Is it because you want to
Yes, maybe
That is so – is so

Love Cannot be Destroyed

Love is an essence that grows
and grows
There is no limit to
its growingness
We imagine we can
diminish it
By a thought, word or deed
Even destroy it
if we try hard
But no matter how much
we try
to extinguish love
It is an impossibility
It cannot be broken
Cannot be contained
Cannot be destroyed
Only in our minds
do we imagine it possible
In the reality of the One Heart
Love conquers all
Love puts a different slant
on our petty tyranny
Love will never end
Love will never be broken
or destroyed
Love is in the heart

The One Heart
It is that it is
Infinite and indestructible
All inclusive
All Heart

ॐ ॐ ॐ

Perhaps You Can Stay

Oft times you come to me
Alone and weary and sore
Tired of the world you live in
Some of you, sometimes
wishing to leave this place
To take your own life
But life can never end
or be ended
If you need to try, then
I will never stop you
You are free to do as you choose
But think on this
and stay a while longer
As I tell you
that however difficult are
your circumstances

Or desperate
And how bad you feel
about yourselves
or others
Or how much pain you have
And believe me
I do know
that it is very, very
difficult at times
But I plead to you
Do not shut me out
Even though you feel you
have never experienced
love
from others or yourself
And are not experiencing it now
And all is darkness
Just ask for love
Not just once
but over and over
And I will come to you
Although sometimes
I have to beat down a door
which is very thick
and padded
and has numerous locks
And whether you ask
in this world or the next

And whether there are a hundred
people, beings
and impediments
blocking your way
And whether you shout or whisper
I am here
I am here
to comfort you
You are not alone
Even though you
think you are
You are never alone
I LOVE YOU
Yes YOU

Skipping into the Arms of Love

Do you remember
skipping merrily down the road
without a care in the world
And sometimes you stumbled and fell
And grazed your knee
Very briefly
a trickle of blood
a sharp pain
and tears
And then you picked yourself up
Or someone else did
and said *there, there*
and put on a plaster
and maybe stroked you
or gave you a kiss
And off you went again
skipping merrily down the road
Quite proud of the plaster
and the scab that formed
before new skin grew again
In fact there was maybe a time
when there was never a time
you didn't have a plaster
or a scab

somewhere or other
What's changed now
Can you go skipping
merrily down the road again
Into the arms of Love
Into the One Heart

༺ ༺ ༺

The Power of Love

When we have been hurt
betrayed and abused
Been made a victim
of other people
of circumstance
and more
Getting in touch with our anger
is a way of regaining our power
And that is good
But beyond that
We can get in touch with a power
beyond our limited selves
A power that is so powerful
It can heal anything
Do anything

The Ultimate Power
which dissolves victimhood
and creates a new way
of being strong
And along with this new power
Comes understanding and compassion
As well as strength beyond measure
Even though
to connect with this power
We need to let go
of everything
Surrender
Yet this is a power that can
move mountains
heal nations
the past
ourselves
The name of this power is love
Unconditionally
Love

EPILOGUE

In the years that have passed
since the book was written
Before I decided to put it out
into the world
Much has changed
with me
and the world
So much change
And through it all
With the help of the One Heart
Is the potential
of a new way
If we are willing
To create a new world of love
A new humanity
Even though things may appear
to get worse
before they get better
Let's do it now
All together
And one at a time
LOVE

INDEX OF POEMS

ABOUT THE AUTHOR

Pam was born in India and, at a young age, came to live in a mining village in Nottinghamshire.

Formally a science teacher, she has worked in the complementary health and spiritual sphere as a healer and therapist for thirty five years, involving her own personal experiences, training and workshops as well as teaching others, and one to one sessions with clients.

Pam and her husband Brian, a nutrition therapist, were involved in various clinics in Kent, before moving to Sheffield where they ran their own residential, teaching and clinic centre. The clinic then moved to the city centre within a health food store before settling in their own premises where they work today.

They have a son who lives in Australia and a daughter who lives close by.

Pam can be contacted through the website: www.thecaringclinic.co.uk

Changing Mindsets & Developing Spirit

Inspirational coaching through verse
for success in sport and life

by Helen K. Emms

Available from Amazon and
www.liveitpublishing.com

There is a force in each of us that compels us to overcome our limitations and strive to experience ourselves and our life at its very best. Yet many of us struggle to be all that we can be. By changing our mind 'sets' and connecting with our Spiritual Self we can finally tap into our awesome inner power to achieve the best in whatever we desire.

Would you like to: Live your life with faith and without fear? Find contentment and deep satisfaction? Tap into your passion, dreams and potential? Develop inner strength, confidence and self-belief? Free yourself to connect with your Spiritual Self? Be who you were born to be? If so this beautifully written book captures the essential qualities and fundamental principles for success in sport and life.

Combining her exceptional expertise in the field of peak performance coaching and personal & spiritual development, with inspirational verse, Helen K Emms coaches us to change disempowering mindsets and nurture our spirit.

An Inner Light
That Shines So Bright

By Liz Everett

**Available from Amazon,
www.liveitpublishing.com
& all good bookshops**

A Heart Warming Collection of Inspirational Writings

An Inner Light That Shines So Bright is a heart-warming collection of inspirational writings that will capture your imagination. Use the powerful words in this remarkable book to:

- Lift your spirits and energise your soul
- Bring comfort, joy, happiness and light into your life
- Enhance personal reflection and meditation
- Encourage your creative inner self to emerge

These emotional and intuitive writings, inspired by Nature, Angels, Faith and Healing amongst others, will touch the heart of everyone in some way.

'Liz shines her light with radiant simplicity, expressing both her sorrow and joy in a way that touched my heart. I felt moved, uplifted and inspired as her experiences resonated with my own, nudging me further forwards on my inner journey.'

Patsi Hayes, Author of Anusha Healing

'These poems cover the spectrum of life: from the joy of nature, to love, faith and painful feelings of loss. I am sure that they will bring insight and inspiration to others who have the pleasure of reading them'.

Dr. Tony Avery, Professor of Primary Care, University of Nottingham

'Liz's passionate poetry is compulsively readable... providing one with an opportunity to read between the lines and hence sending them on the profound journey of self-discovery.'

Dr. Eva Carlton Ph.D. BSc (Hons) Psychology

Attention Writers

Get published!

Everyone has a book inside of them. If you have the passion and determination to get it out there and tell the world, we can help you.

LIP works with new and established authors in the fields of:

- Personal Development, Self-Help, Popular Psychology & NLP
- Health, Healing & Alternative Therapies
- Motivational, Inspirational & Spiritual
- Business, Management & Entrepreneurship

We want to help you turn your creative work into reality!

Our innovative and progressive multi-media partnership publishing house will help you live the dream by getting your books, e-books, Ds and MP3s professionally published and distributed across a global network.

For more information visit our website at:

www.**liveitpublishing**.com

LIP... The easiest way to get published!